D0882229

What'sNext?

Real Estate
in the
New Economy

Urban Land Institute

SEVENTY-FIVE YEARS OF
BUILDING COMMUNITY

Recommended Bibliographic Listing:
Urban Land Institute. *What's Next? Real Estate in the New Economy.*
Washington, D.C.: Urban Land Institute, 2011

International Standard Book Number: 978-0-87420-164-2

ULI Order #W22

Cover photo: Terry Vine/Stone/
Getty Images

Support and Sponsorship

The Urban Land Institute gratefully acknowledges the leadership and support of UDR, Inc.

UDR, Inc. (NYSE:UDR), an S&P 400 company, is a leading multifamily real estate investment trust with a demonstrated performance history of delivering superior and dependable returns by successfully managing, buying, selling, developing and redeveloping attractive real estate properties in targeted U.S. markets. UDR is honored to celebrate with ULI its 75th commemorative year. As a proud long-term sponsor of ULI we recognize the industry-leading research, education, and community outreach efforts of ULI and its goal of providing participants with thoughtful analysis, spirited debate, and industry best practices. UDR is grateful for the forum ULI has provided the Company to facilitate the open exchange of ideas and information as well as the sharing of experience with other local, national, and multinational industry leaders.

The Urban Land Institute recognizes the following supporters as ULI 75th Anniversary sponsors:

Additional support provided by:

About the Urban Land Institute

The Urban Land Institute is a 501(c)(3) nonprofit research and education organization supported by its members. Founded in 1936, the Institute now has members in 95 countries worldwide, representing the entire spectrum of land use and real estate development disciplines working in private enterprise and public service.

As the preeminent multidisciplinary real estate forum, ULI facilitates an open exchange of ideas, information, and experience among local, national, and international industry leaders and policy makers dedicated to creating better places.

The mission of the Urban Land Institute is to provide leadership in the responsible use of land and in creating and sustaining thriving communities worldwide. ULI is committed to

- Bringing together leaders from across the fields of real estate and land use policy to exchange best practices and serve community needs;

- Fostering collaboration within and beyond ULI's membership through mentoring, dialogue, and problem solving;

- Exploring issues of urbanization, conservation, regeneration, land use, capital formation, and sustainable development;

- Advancing land use policies and design practices that respect the uniqueness of both build and natural environments;

- Sharing knowledge through education, applied research, publishing, and electronic media; and

- Sustaining a diverse global network of local practice and advisory efforts that address current and future challenges.

ULI's priorities are

- Promoting intelligent densification and urbanization;

- Creating resilient communities;

- Understanding demand and market forces;

- Connecting capital and the built environment through value; and

- Integrating energy, resources, and uses sustainably.

Table of Contents

Dear Reader:

At the 2011 ULI Fall Meeting, the Urban Land Institute kicks off its 75th birthday celebration. Building on a legacy rooted in a handful of landowners sharing best practices during the Great Depression, ULI has grown to nearly 30,000 members worldwide, over 65 local district councils, and offices in Washington, D.C.; London; Tokyo; and Hong Kong. A nonprofit organization, ULI has become the premier source of multidisciplinary research and education in the real estate industry. Serving private investors, lenders, developers, owners, service providers, and public officials alike, ULI is a welcoming safe haven for all market participants to engage in dialogue, debate, and analysis of market trends and future challenges facing urban markets locally and globally.

As we embark on the next 75 years of ULI activities, we all understand that the investment outlook for America's single largest financial asset class is critical to broader economic recovery and essential to building and sustaining thriving communities. Over the next year, ULI will engage in a broad dialogue bridging the market realities of today with the land use outcomes of tomorrow. Through the passsionate involvement of local communities and serious reflection on professional practice at national and international events, ULI will explore *What's Next? Real Estate in the New Economy*. At the ULI Fall Meeting in 2012, we will gather and present the findings in a business-oriented perspective, summarizing the anniversary year information, dialogue, and engagement.

For the first time in human history, more people are living in cities. The world is urbanizing as never before, bringing both opportunity and peril. Metropolitan areas must address population diversity, respond to natural disasters, and encourage creativity, leadership, and problem solving. The way communities tackle new challenges ripples into the future, creating long-term opportunities and constraints. ULI is uniquely poised to take stock of existing real estate markets and look forward into the next era of urban development and economics, when new paradigms will shape investments in both infrastructure and property. *What's Next?* seeks to challenge ULI members to reframe the nature of the real estate marketplace by looking forward to 2020.

Communities in the United States and around the world struggle to adapt to and cope with changing markets, real estate and the values underpinning the world's great urban centers. This coming decade presents a pivot point for the cumulative endeavors of community building. More than ever before in the long history of urbanization, economic, demographic, and environmental factors are coming together to elevate the importance of land use in meeting residents' and businesses' expectations for livability, amenities, mobility, and ongoing sustainability. Overwhelmingly, global markets are being driven by what happens in urban areas. Yet great cities are not just centers of commercial activity. Great cities are about what's best for people and their social interaction. Around the world, the communities that get this right will be the winners of the future.

We hope this publication spurs a constructive dialogue in your community.

Sincerely,

Peter S. Rummell
Chairman

Patrick L. Phillips
Chief Executive Officer

Sometimes decades hang on for more than ten years.

The introduction to the 21st century is still unfolding in cities and communities around the world. The complexity of the Great Recession continues to challenge all market players with implications that ripple out across countries, industries, currencies, and communities. From reconstruction dilemmas following natural disasters to civil unrest, political friction, and the heart-stopping ravages of the latest famine, we feel a world getting smaller yet more complicated and interdependent than ever before.

After decades of what felt like infinite resources and vast wealth pools available to fuel the consumption-based U.S. economy, we now face a mindset of shortage. We all know the history—government-supported mortgages and freeways, affordable automobiles, cheap gas, and post–World War II industrial expansion all underwrote the exodus from "cramped" urban neighborhoods to spacious single-family suburban homes. Car models were a talisman for individual success, and public transit turned into an afterthought in suburban agglomerations. Proximity to anything didn't matter when you could drive easily to almost everywhere. And exhilarating mobility over long distances enabled more people to own more land—and build larger houses—at the ever-expanding suburban fringe. Employers sought to build suburban office islands, set apart from housing, retail, and transit.

That's over. What's next?

As we preview the future, three critical forces drive change:

Accelerating Globalization—From energy to food to manufacturing, the metrics of globalization shed light on the rise and fall of global markets on a 24/7 basis as cities around the world ebb and flow with massive capital investments and withdrawals. Burgeoning and shrinking cities mirror investors' search for lower costs of production and optimum locations for both manufacturing and services. Our social networks and governance structures struggle to keep pace and adapt quickly and creatively to process all of the input that various interests want and need to give. Disparities between rich and poor expand, uncertainty and lack of confidence grow, and prognosticators hyperventilate with fears of the future.

Changing Demographics—The rapidly evolving social composition of communities has a more powerful reach and not only reframes a neighborhood or a state but also triggers new markets, new opportunities, and new products and services. Immigration produces not just a plethora of diverse restaurants in virtually every town and suburb, but also new residents vying for jobs, housing, and a toehold on the ladder of success. The "barbell" population groups of the Boomers and Generation Y challenge the markets, from where and how we live and work, to how we learn, heal, and relax.

Ever-Evolving Technologies—Technology is pushing more information into the marketplace and onto our smartphones at warp speed. We can monitor and manage our activities, our navigation, and every value proposition with ever more accuracy and in real time. The community-building potential of communications technology is on a meteoric catapult across the globe, replacing entire industries along the way. Whether to detect underperforming heating, ventilation, and air-conditioning equipment, monitor the arrival of the next bus, or catalyze political engagement, communities and businesses are exploring the power of instant connectivity for good or ill.

These underlying forces will combine with many others in indeterminate ways over the coming years. In the world of real estate investment, the continual challenge is to understand new trends, capitalize on new market opportunities, and direct investment funds in strategic ways. No time in recent memory has been as complex or as subject to detailed analysis as our current time—or changing as rapidly.

It's all about thinking in a different way.

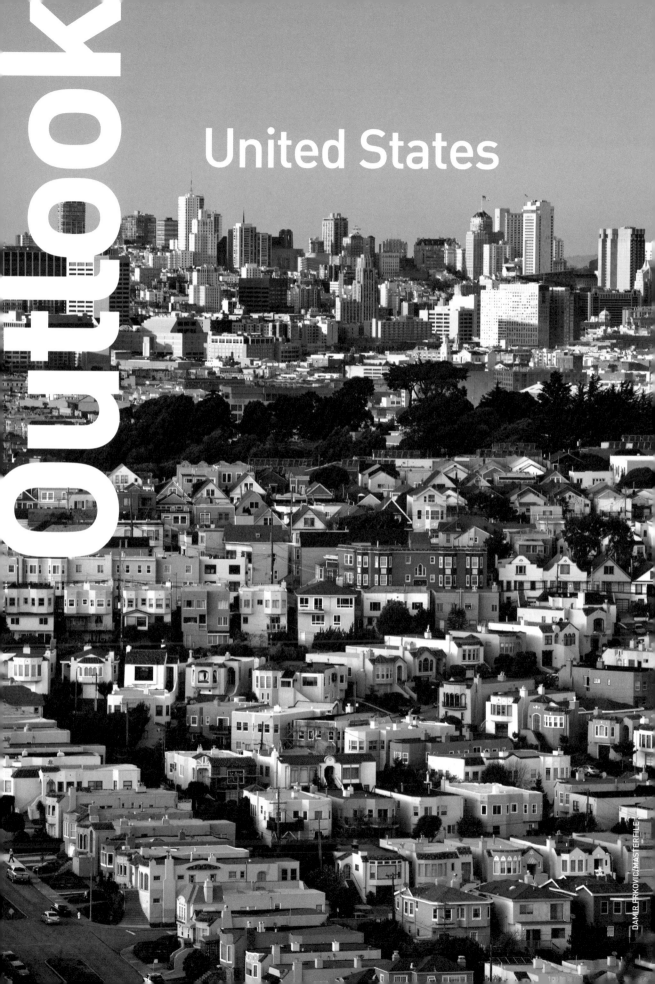

United States

New Hurdles

For the immediate future, American consumers will come to grips with the discomfiting and considerable uncertainty involved in reaching limits that have been exposed by the deep recession, the credit crisis, and the impacts of global competition for jobs. A large borrowing bill has come due, forcing government retrenchment and individual belt-tightening; almost all stakeholders must deleverage. The foreclosure crisis and plummeting home values present the most obvious object lesson. Stubborn unemployment levels are pushing increasing numbers of Americans, especially Gen Yers, to consider where and how they find satisfactory work and an affordable life.

Cross-Currents and Undertows

Several fundamental economic and demographic drivers will dramatically influence real estate investment and urban development over the current decade. Here is what future investors and developers face:

Global Networks—Increasingly, market prospects rise and fall in response to an ever more interdependent world economy where emerging economies gain clout, boost demand, and generate new business. Commercial activity will continue to organize around the network of gateway cities that form a series of global pathways. Major international airports and seaports allow employers, enabled by new technology, to outsource more service sector and manufacturing jobs to lower-cost places and continue to replace workers with ever more sophisticated machines. An evolving network of primary, secondary, and tertiary relationships take shape to capitalize on value creation in global emerging markets.

Rightsizing—Conspicuous consumption takes a hit for all but a narrow few. Real estate offers an obvious target for reducing expenses—smaller occupied spaces cost less to own, rent, heat, cool, furnish, and maintain. Office tenants decrease space per employee, looking for more efficiency and productivity. Retailers employ logistics strategies and fully integrate online and in-store options to limit both floor and storage space.

Homeownership drops, and more people want the convenience of living closer to work.

Job Generators Shift—Manufacturing continues its decades-long relocation from older factories in higher-cost union states in the Northeast and Midwest either to new plants built in right-to-work states in the South and Southwest or entirely out of the country. A new generation of "advanced manufacturing" creeps into select markets, breathing new life into communities that have found their voice in a global niche, albeit with lower levels of employment than the old "smokestacks." Northern cities like Boston and Pittsburgh build on their knowledge industries of education and medical institutions—"eds and meds"—and continue to replace manufacturing jobs with new science, technology, and health care–related specialties.

The Education Magnet—The dramatic differences in education levels across markets becomes a major driver in location, not just for businesses but for residents as well. In West Virginia, Arkansas, and Nevada, only 24 percent of young adults have

World's Busiest Airports by Number of Passengers, 2010

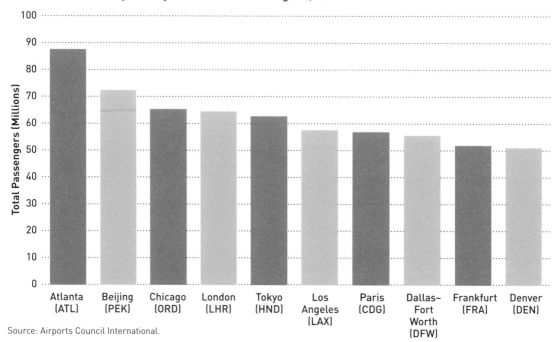

Source: Airports Council International.

some form of postsecondary education, where in Massachusetts, Minnesota, and North Dakota more than 44 percent of the same population has a college degree. Businesses choose communities with higher education rates; recent graduates are attracted by the good jobs, industry clusters, and specializations which naturally occur. Which city do you want on your resume? Whether the Bay Area for high-tech or the Baltimore-Washington corridor for bioscience, the regional market winners of the next decade are evident today.

Demographics Become Destiny

The mix of people who occupy our buildings and form our communities is going through a dramatic change:

Gen Y Arrives—The largest demographic age cohort in the United States—ranging from the teens through the early thirties—is technologically savvy, highly mobile, and hungry to build careers while delaying families. They gravitate to more urban places looking for jobs and crave interactive

Share of U.S. Labor Force by Age Group (Percent)

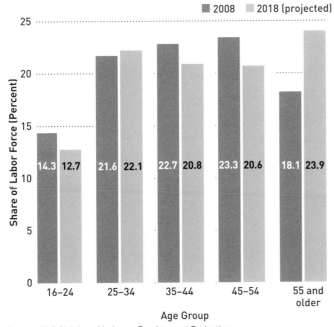

Source: BLS Division of Industry Employment Projections.

environments that nurture social diversity and fun. They prefer flexible working situations, want to live in stimulating neighborhoods, and don't mind dealing with less individual space. At the same time, new immigrants and less well-educated young people seek places that allow financial and cultural growth.

Workers Face More Dependents—Demographically, the percentage of working-age Americans decreases as the traditional non-working-age population (younger than 20 and older than 65) grows. That means each working American supports more dependents, stressing family resources. Intergenerational living increases as more families pool assets to help each other make ends meet. Large houses don't necessarily go out of fashion for everyone. More creative cohabitation arrangements arise as friends and acquaintances stretch available dollars and credit.

Flying Solo—More households consist of a single person—27 percent by 2020. The rise in women living alone creates a new demographic segment seeking greater security and amenities.

Diversity Increases—Meanwhile, the ascendancy of the Hispanic population in the United States continues, moving toward 50 million persons. Many metropolitan areas become "minority majority" communities as Asian, African American, and Hispanic populations surpass the traditional caucasian majorities.

Extended Employment (Not Retirement)—Cash-strapped seniors may need to work longer. Some 40 percent of Boomers say they don't have enough savings for retirement. Many may not leave existing jobs or existing hard-to-sell homes to relocate to familiar retirement bastions in warm-weather Sunbelt locales. The momentum of the graying Boomers will ramp up the perceived demand for senior housing. The number of seniors over age 80 grows rapidly. As they live longer than ever before, their ability to afford their longer lives is problematic. So as the senior population grows faster than any other age group, the percentage of them able to afford dedicated facilities declines, and many more age in place by choice or move in with relatives.

Hitting Limits

A new recognition of market constraints shape urban investment strategies:

Rising Transportation Costs—Mobility suddenly costs more—at the pump, in lost time, and in higher tolls. Amid increased global demand for oil from new economic powers, the price of gasoline heads higher. Ubiquitous automobile congestion begins to strangle economic hubs in productivity-sapping paralysis as concerns intensify about the impacts of climate change from fossil fuel emissions. Demand grows for locations and real estate that provide a combined live-work solution, enabling people to drive less or have the ability to pursue a more "virtual" work-from-home occupation.

Infrastructure Deficits—Public sector shortfalls curtail spending on repairing, rebuilding, and repurposing existing transportation infrastructure. Increasingly outmoded 20th-century systems like the once-vaunted interstate highways struggle to handle the demands of burgeoning populations and changing

Supporting Workers per Social Security Beneficiary, 1945–2030

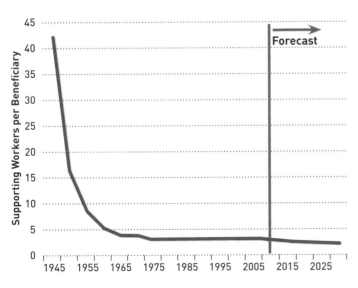

In 1945, each retiree was supported by 42 workers, compared with three workers in 2009.

Source: Social Security Administration.

logistics. The United States falls behind Asia and Europe in developing efficient mass transit and freight-hauling networks, potentially short-circuiting productivity and mobility. Private capital and creative partnerships have an opportunity to fill the void and team up with local government to overcome these problems. New urban experimentation emerges as market demand for high-quality place making is met through public/private partnerships and opportunistic privatization of public services.

Water Extremes—Some fast-growing states, especially in the South, Southwest, and West, confront growing challenges from inadequate water supplies and rigid frameworks for water rights. These arid areas, including a swath from Colorado and Texas west to California, cannot sustain population trends in cur-

San Francisco put Valencia Street on a "road diet" by removing two car lanes and installing bike lanes and a median. As a result, bike traffic increased by 144 percent, motor vehicle traffic decreased by 10 percent, and 66 percent of merchants said the redesign improved business.

SAN FRANCISCO BICYCLE COALITION, CONNECTING THE CITY PROJECT

rent drier-than-normal conditions. Savvy developers and owners gain an edge by embracing water-saving technologies and landscaping. In spot areas from North Dakota to New Orleans, spikes of too much water from floods and storms pose greater problems. Flood mitigation and risk assessment grow in importance as public sector actors can no longer subsidize owners.

New Opportunities

While the United States endures this rough patch, Americans can neither afford to despair over a slow jobs recovery nor assume that good times will return as they always have in the past. The decade ahead presents new opportunities to generate profitable outcomes by realistically facing change in increasingly segmented economic markets, repositioning to take advantage of altered demand, and employing new technologies and creative development strategies.

For the real estate industry, it's a time to rethink and evolve, reinvent and renew. Metropolitan areas in the United States represent over 80 percent of the gross domestic product (GDP) of the country and over 80 percent of the population. Nearly 100 percent of robust population growth is located in urban areas. Metropolitan growth is embracing a new mixture of land uses, new suburban centers, and in-town reconfigurations. There is a new focus on leveraging existing employment centers by elevating the role of education and medical clusters as engines of growth.

Despite difficult challenges, the United States retains the key attributes and wealth stores needed to drive a globally competitive economy with an innovation edge. Lifestyles adjust as Americans redefine "the good life" and reformulate their American Dream. The country's unmatched legal system, premier universities, transparent and free markets, effective regulation, creative culture, and substantial capital reserves still engender the world's most fertile environment for entrepreneurship. Economic declines historically have been met by resilience and regeneration-producing new companies and industries, some growing into global leaders.

That can happen again.

Work

Where the hell are

NATIONAL
CareerFairs
making connections face to face

CAREER FAIR

the **jobs?**

Work

Where the hell are the **jobs?**

How will the evolving employment markets drive real estate decisions? How is the knowledge economy affecting communities?

Proximity to Global Pathways, Leveraging Brainpower

As the world of work morphs—as companies rethink where they locate and double down on productivity strategies—many under-educated and undertrained Americans are discovering ever-narrowing options for landing high-paying jobs. Not since the elevator's invention moved businesses out of walk-ups and into vertical towers has anything like the ongoing virtual revolution altered concepts of how to deploy people and operate businesses in what's become a truly global marketplace. In the real estate world, investors and developers naturally follow jobs as new networks form between consolidating business power centers—a relative handful of 24-hour global gateways. The prospects for secondary and tertiary markets turn on how well they capitalize on anchor institution assets and skill clusters.

Centers aggregating government, universities, and medical complexes provide the ingredients for incubating entrepreneurial activity and generating tech and biotech startups fed by research grants and academic talent. For communities to thrive, education and a cluster of talented firms, workers, government leaders, and local amenities are required. Not surprisingly,

Investments by Selected Industry, Q1 2011 ($ Millions)

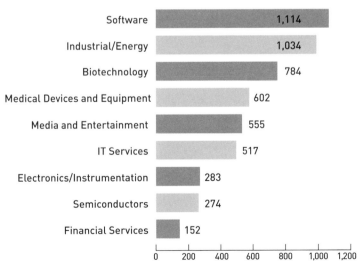

Industry	$ Millions
Software	1,114
Industrial/Energy	1,034
Biotechnology	784
Medical Devices and Equipment	602
Media and Entertainment	555
IT Services	517
Electronics/Instrumentation	283
Semiconductors	274
Financial Services	152

Source: PwC.

What's next?

- Technology Transfer

- Health Care Clusters

- Education, Education, Education

- Advanced Manufacturing

- Global Pathways

places with a high percentage of well-educated residents have grown the fastest and experienced less pain during the current recession. Unemployment in the highly educated metropolitan areas has averaged 2 to 3 percent lower than the national average and significantly lower than those communities with a less well-educated workforce.

The continuing move to high-tech and medical businesses persists. Within the first quarter of 2011, over $6 billion was invested in new high-tech and medical industries. Venture capital dollars have fueled the growth in tech-rich places. In 2007 alone, over $10 billion in venture funding went into the San Jose, San Francisco, and Berkeley corridor. The ability of universities to successfully encourage technology transfer and commercial development of their research is a recruiting tool for both faculty and students and a strong indicator of community prosperity. Treasure Island in San Francisco is building over 2,000 homes, attracting 2,500 to 3,000 permanent jobs and as many as 2,000 construction jobs as it builds out. At Candlestick Point, development expectations include over 12,000 new housing units and over 3 million square feet (279,000 sq m) of new office and research and development space.

Top Ten Metropolitan Areas by Number of College Degrees

Rank	Metropolitan Area	Proportion of Residents with Degrees (Percent)
1	Washington, DC	47.3
2	San Francisco	43.5
3	San Jose	43.2
4	Raleigh	42.2
5	Boston	42.2
6	Austin	38.7
7	Minneapolis	37.6
8	Denver	37.6
9	Seattle	37.4
10	New York	35.6

Source: U.S. Census Bureau.

Despite the current downturn, the Bureau of Labor Statistics projects strong growth in professional services, service sector, and construction jobs over the next ten years. This mirrors industry data and reflects the increase in health services, education, and information-related employment. While manufacturing employment has declined by 20 to 40 percent or more over the past 20 years, in many markets these jobs have been replaced by dramatic increases in employment in professional and business services as well as education and health services. The unfortunate part of this change is the frequent mismatch between the skills of the manufacturing worker and the skills required by the new jobs in the professional and skilled services ranks.

Redefining Assets

As the new economy emerges, a deep understanding of community assets and growth prospects is needed. Population trends by segment, jobs analysis and trends, and an understanding of the major educational and medical institutions

Top 25 U.S. Metropolitan Statistical Areas in the Biosciences

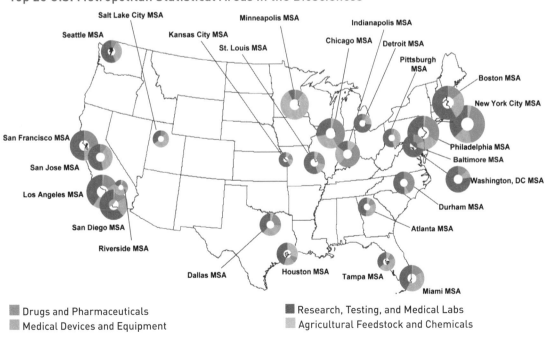

- ■ Drugs and Pharmaceuticals
- ■ Medical Devices and Equipment
- ■ Research, Testing, and Medical Labs
- ■ Agricultural Feedstock and Chemicals

Source: Battelle/BIO State Biosciences Initiatives 2010.

in a community is required. Local leadership and willingness to create innovative public/private partnerships, strategically invest in new infrastructure, and open doors for young people with affordable housing and entry-level jobs are keys to sustaining thriving communities.

Manufacturing Moves Forward

What's left of the nation's manufacturing businesses remains strong, albeit at their present reduced levels, and becomes ever more technologically sophisticated. Some continue the decades-long migration from rusting northern industrial citadels to cheaper labor markets—typically warmer, right-to-work states or entirely out of the country—while others stay in niche labor markets where the best skilled workers are to be found. There are some bright notes on the manufacturing front: digital design and laser construction are adding employment and retooling parts of Europe's labor force in the United Kingdom and Germany, keeping some small communities on the global map. The United States can harness these techniques.

Number of U.S. Job Openings Due to Growth and Replacement Needs, by Major Occupational Group, 2008–2018

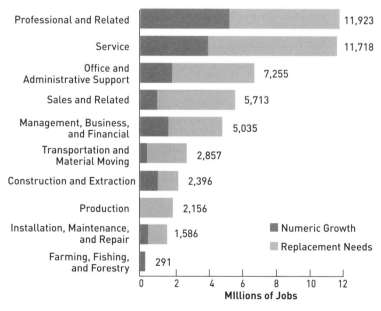

Source: BLS Division of Occupational Outlook.

Under the best circumstances advanced robotics and automation temper any major expansion of factory-based jobs but may offer select opportunities in some markets. Creating specialized and custom products within the United States becomes easier and less expensive. Smaller companies that specialize in "mass customization" are expanding, and demanding new skill sets, job training programs, and economic development efforts.

The Triangle (Raleigh, Durham, and Chapel Hill) is home to nearly 60 companies and 3,000 employees working in various aspects of the smart grid industry. The digital power grid is expected to replace the nation's aging mechanical grid over the next decade, giving regional smart grid hubs like the Triangle an economic edge in high-paying technology jobs for what will become an essential service.

THE RESEARCH TRIANGLE PARK

Accounting for Natural Resources

Ample water resources remain a long-term trump card for northern states—they have plenty of it and manufacturers and power companies need water to thrive. Many Sunbelt regions, especially in the dry Southwest and even in the moister Southeast, appear water challenged, which could constrain future factory expansions. Wind and biomass resources have geographies of their own. The perception of natural resource abundance may alter community investment decisions.

Securing Anchors: Eds and Meds

Government, academia, and hospitals form a powerful combination of attractions to buck up places that have been left off global pathways. Despite the recent budget cutting and layoffs, government continues to provide a measure of stability to any city lucky enough to have a concentration of public employee jobs.

Cleveland, Ohio, is striving to become a leader in the biomedical field through an existing hub of medical imaging, pharmaceutical developers and bioscience researchers, and the presence of the Cleveland Clinic and Case Western Reserve University. Since 2001, the number of biomedical firms in the area has more than doubled, to 600. Venture capital investments have swelled to an average of $150 million a year since 2005, versus $30 million a year from 1996 to 2001. The planned Cleveland Medical Mart & Convention Center will be the world's first marketplace for medical industry buyers and sellers.

"Far and away the best prize that life has to offer is the chance to work hard at **work** worth doing."

—Franklin Delano Roosevelt

Just look at the ultimate government center, Washington, D.C., perennially the country's most dependable commercial real estate market. Add in a major university or two, as well as a large hospital complex and specialized cancer or heart disease treatment facility, and a smaller city has the makings of a diversified jobs generator with potential for breakthroughs in developing new tech, biotech, and alternative energy–related businesses.

Austin and Raleigh-Durham anchor their favored smaller-market status in eds, meds, and feds formulas that leverage institutions. Denver, Phoenix, and Nashville, three other Sunbelt capitals, appear to capitalize on this concept too. These metropolitan environments appeal to the most attractive segments of the two biggest population cohorts—recent college graduates, who hunger for exciting and remunerative employment, and wealthy seniors, who hanker for stimulating academic environments and the availability of top-flight doctors and medical facilities.

Health care, resort, and senior living industries in familiar warm-weather bastions like Florida and Arizona as well as more temperate states like the Carolinas, Colorado, and Utah continue to garner their share of business from snowbirds and retirees relocating for easier lifestyles.

Real estate development skews more to the extremes: higher-end condo/resort community projects and hotels tailored to Boomers living off accumulated assets, as well as downscale workforce housing—particularly apartments and embedded neighborhood retail—for lower-paid health care and service sector employees tending to the aging population's needs.

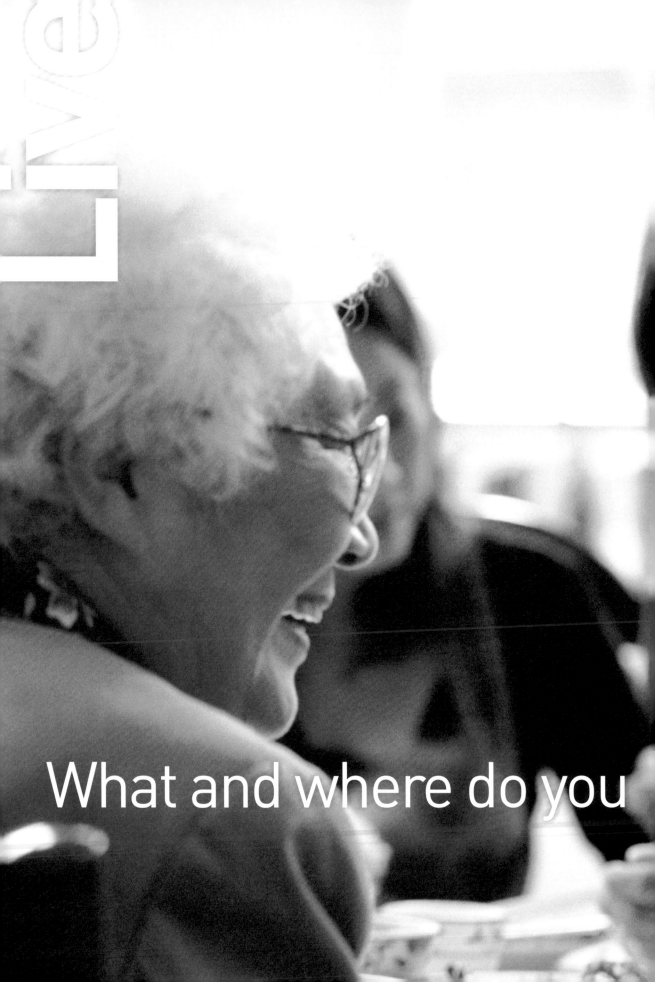

Live

What and where do you

call **home?**

Live

What and where do you call **home?**

What will household
composition look like?
How do thrift and the
good life come together?

More People in Less Space

Well, it was nice while it lasted. Young adults getting out of college or working at their first job could rent a place and then, in a few years, buy a starter home. Their parents aged into empty nesters living in their own space, while retired grandparents with

National House Price Indicators, 2006–2011 (Percent Change)

Country	July 2011	Q1 2010	2006–2011	Under (-)/over(+) valued[a]
Hong Kong	23.9	30.3	96	+63.7
Singapore	10.1	25.1	63	+17.3
France	8.7	1.4	11	+48.5
Belgium	5.5	5.1	22	+20.5
Switzerland	4.4	4.9	18	+5.5
China	3.9	10.6	34	+13.9
Denmark	2.2	1.3	-10	+18.3
Sweden	2.1	10.7	25	+35.8
Canada	2.0	1.9	13	+21.2
Germany	0.9	-0.7	-4	-12.8
Australia	-0.2	18.8	33	+50.1
South Africa	-0.3	10.2	29	—
Britain	-1.2	9.1	0	+27.8
Italy	-1.6	-3.4	1	+8.7
New Zealand	-1.6	6.4	6.0	+17.6
Netherlands	-2.1	6.0	-4	+16.9
United States (Case-Shiller ten-city index)	-3.1	1.5	-32	-0.5
United States (FHFA)	-3.1	-6.4	-13	+4.8
Japan	-3.3	-4.0	-12	-35.8
Spain	-4.7	-4.7	-9	+39.2
United States (Case-Shiller national index)	-5.1	2.3	-33	-11.4
Ireland	-12.2	-16.6	-35	+22.9

Note: — = not available. FHFA = Federal Housing Finance Agency.
a. Against long-run average of price-to-rents ratio.
Source: "Rooms with a view." *The Economist*. July 7, 2011.

What's next?

- Rental Housing
- Aging in Place
- Multigenerational Households
- Understanding Your Tenant
- Mortgage Reform

generous pensions and government entitlements could live in-dependently, many moving to some warm-weather spot far from the kids. Everybody could afford to be on their own in their own place. But that's just no longer the case for many of us.

Average compensation in the United States had been leveling off or sliding even before the recession; private pensions have been abrogated for many workers; and more retirements rely shak-ily on self-managed 401(k) s or just Social Security. Diminished home values have broken many family nest eggs. This isn't going to change during this decade, which means that affordability—always a key element in housing markets—is taking on a whole new meaning as developers reach for ways to make attractive homes within the means of financially constrained buyers.

What does all this mean?

To save money, more of us must either live in larger households or in smaller units. Looking on the brighter side, the American family has a chance to reconnect, and what's wrong with that?

Growth in Renter Households by Age Group, 2010–2020

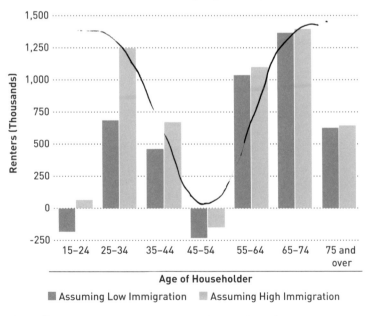

Source: "The State of the Nation's Housing 2010." The Joint Center for Housing Studies of Harvard University.

All signs point to more Americans renting and a further decline in homeownership as defaults on mortgages and foreclosures continue. Tight lending standards (buyers now actually need equity and sound credit histories) keep many folks who should never have been purchasing in the first place out of the market. Existing apartment owners—you are golden. Multifamily demand swells—more people move back into rental units, vacancies decline, and rents ratchet up. Institutional investors increasingly make apartments their much preferred property sector, hoping for more predictable, solid returns with lower risk.

Multifamily developers reemerge from hibernation and start building again. Six million new renter households may be

Quincy, Massachusetts, is planning to rebuild 50 acres of its aging downtown core. When complete, it is designed to include approximately 1,400 multifamily residential units, two hotels, 750,000 square feet of retail, and over 1 million square feet of office space. The $1.6 billion project is being financed as a public/private partnership.

STREET-WORKS LLC

formed between 2008 and 2015, requiring 300,000 new units annually compared with just 100,000 in 2010. But can the industry deliver that amount for the rents at which people looking to rent can afford? Keep in mind that more single-family homes will turn into rentals as loan servicers, investors, and speculators lease properties until the for-sale market turns around. In any case, homebuilders probably remain on an enforced siesta until mid-decade. At some point, rising rents and lowered home prices flip some renters back into homebuyers as select forms of product hit the market, such as new infill attached units, which provide an alternative to new product being delivered in traditional land subdivisions.

Suburban Lifestyles Evolve

Apartment projects concentrate at mass transit stations and near suburban town centers, gradually turning single-use commercial strips into mixed-use corridors. Community planners and local governments have the opportunity to work with developers in fashioning more multi-use town center concepts around existing shopping malls and office nodes.

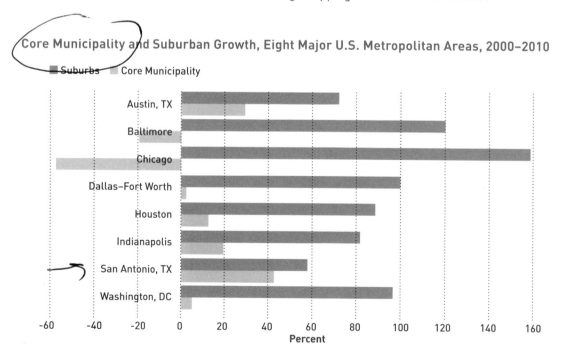

Core Municipality and Suburban Growth, Eight Major U.S. Metropolitan Areas, 2000–2010

■ Suburbs   ■ Core Municipality

Source: "The Still Elusive 'Return to the City,'" Wendell Cox, February 22, 2011.

These projects can meet intensifying demand for live-work environments which involve less car dependency and feature walkable neighborhoods, features which are very attractive to the
increasing share of single-person households who make "living
solo" a way of life. In turn, more compact development—involv-
ing high- and mid-rise buildings as well as townhouses—bolster
continuing urbanizing trends in many suburban locations.

Different Living Configurations

New apartments and apartment building makeovers should
cater to a range of niche renters who may want more space
rather than less—including extended families and residents
who require home offices. The in-law suite adds real value but
may be occupied by recent college graduates. In rethinking
indoor space, residential developers and owners should consider fewer hallways, smaller bedrooms, large kitchens open-
ing onto a family space, and big living room space for groups
congregating around TV and movie entertainment. Club rooms
and shared recreation facilities like rooftop pools and workout

**U.S. Population Living in Multigenerational Family
Households, 1940–2008**

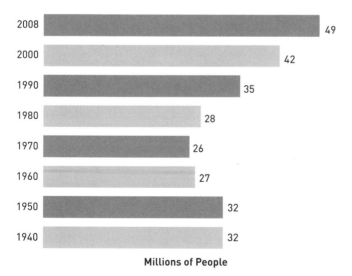

Millions of People

Sources: Pew Research Center analysis of U.S. Decennial Census data, 1940–2000,
and 2006, 2007, 2008 American Community Surveys, based on Integrated Public Use
Microdata Series (IPUMS) samples.

rooms become more coveted. Pedestrian access to restaurants, cafes, and parks or recreation centers adds real value.

Meanwhile, more single-family homes are occupied by renters changing the feel and politics of suburban communities. Today, 14 percent of households are multigenerational families, a share that will undoubtedly increase, especially as inner-city and new immigrant households opt for suburban neighborhoods. In the banner years of the past decade, over 2 million homes were produced. Going forward, don't expect more than 1 million new homes per year—and that happens only once the markets are back, after several more years.

Projected Growth in Population Age 65 and Older by State, 2010–2020 (Percent)

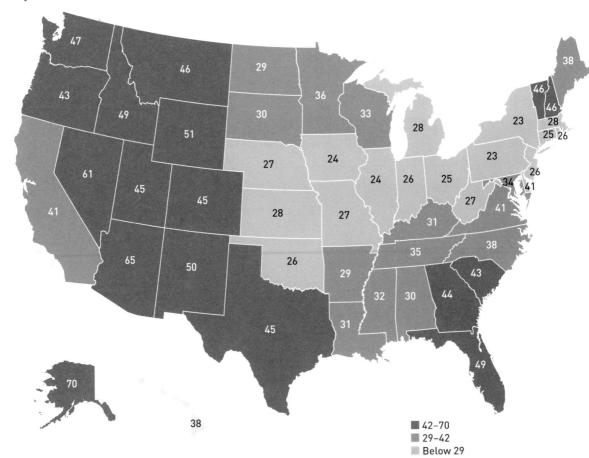

Legend:
- 42–70
- 29–42
- Below 29

Source: Brookings Institute analysis of 2010 Census Bureau population projections.

Although monster McMansions go the way of Hummers, ample-sized suburban homes may come back into vogue sooner than we think. Houses with multiple bedrooms and bathrooms are well suited to accommodate an expected increase in multigenerational living arrangements, as more families pool resources. Grandparents facing shrinking retirement savings or forced into early retirement can take care of grandkids, eliminating child care costs, while both parents work to help make ends meet. Adult kids, some married and with children, move back in with parents and stay longer as well-paying jobs become harder to land. Immigrant families—Hispanic, East and South Asian, African, Russian—characteristically open their homes to relatives and friends of relatives as they gain economic footholds. When you add multiple incomes together, houses at lower price points may become reasonable and monthly mortgage payments possible. Various forms of "doubling up" —cohabitation, roommate, and sibling living arrangements—will incubate, too.

Today, 14 percent of households are multigenerational families, a proportion that will undoubtedly increase as inner-city and new immigrant households opt for suburban neighborhoods.

FUSE/GETTY IMAGES

The Gray Wave's Changing Profile

For years developers of senior housing have anticipated the leading edge of graying Boomers, now finally reaching the 65-year milestone. Although sheer numbers mean more business, many Boomers may not have an interest in retirement housing for another decade and may stay in the workforce longer. Older seniors may not have the means to make such moves. Lengthening lifespans and crimped savings could mean that more elderly outlive resources, creating issues for operators. The gray wave toward warmer-weather destinations like Arizona, Florida, and the Carolinas likely continues but possibly with reduced intensity as more seniors age in place or move in or near children and grandchildren.

Wanting Varied Options

Those affluent 50- and 60-something empty nesters continue to downsize out of larger suburban homes (if they don't have underwater homes trapping them in place), looking for more convenient urban lifestyles. Easier-to-take-care-of condo-

Fastest-Growing Senior Populations: Top Ten U.S. Metropolitan Areas

Rank	Metropolitan Area	Proportion of Population Age 65 and Older in 2010 (Percent)	Increase in People Age 65 and Older, 2000–2010 (Percent)
1	Raleigh, NC	9.0	60
2	Austin, TX	8.1	53
3	Las Vegas	11.3	50
4	Boise, ID	10.9	46
5	Atlanta	9.0	44
6	Provo, UT	6.5	42
7	Colorado Springs, CO	10.1	40
8	Houston	8.6	39
9	Dallas	8.8	38
10	Charlotte, NC	10.1	36

Source: U.S. Census 2010.

miniums and townhouses work for them. Those with financial cushions support second-home markets in resort and vacation destinations, though at diminished levels. Others may look to move closer to (although not in with) children and grandchildren. For those able to seek senior residences, health and wellness programs rank as top priorities along with urban, walkable settings, public transportation, and connectivity. Elderly parents and their children want and use more smart technologies to help maintain self-sufficiency and monitor health status. Since many other still-healthy seniors prefer to avoid the perceived stigma of "retirement communities," developers could take advantage by converting condos into "age-friendly" residences with concierge services and optional in-home assistance, including meal preparation.

Urban Action, Gateway Attraction

Overwhelmingly, bright-light urban environments attract the exploding number of career-building, Boomer offspring known as Generation Y. After rooming in college dorms, these 20-somethings on tight budgets prefer places to congregate with friends—in parks, bar scenes, restaurant clusters, and building common areas—and can tolerate smaller living spaces. Priced out of many in-town neighborhoods, this generation willingly settles for less pricey digs in urbanizing commercial nodes along transit routes convenient to center-city

Marital Status at Age 18–28, by Generation, United States (Percent)

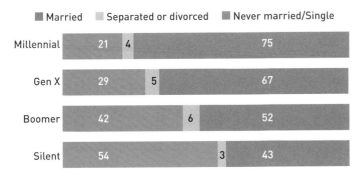

Source: Pew Research Center tabulations from the March Current Population Surveys (1963, 1978, 1995, and 2009) for the civilian, noninstitutional population.

jobs. They delay marrying and leave the more sedate, suburban, child-rearing scene to the older, "baby buster" Generation X, now in their thirties and early forties. In the near term, this other relatively small demographic cohort cannot sustain the same demand levels for suburban housing as the much larger cohort of Boomers.

Upscale neighborhoods in prime gateway cities remain magnets for business elites and wealthy retirees as long as crime rates stay low. Unique and sought-after 24-hour amenities—cultural institutions, entertainment districts, shopping attractions, tourist destinations, and superior mass transit infrastructure—increase demand, while geographical and development barriers to entry limit supply. Businesses congregate in these cities, attracted by the confluence of interacting brainpower and access to global pathways through major international airports.

Big jobs and bigger paychecks lure the best and the brightest to gateway locations, supporting premium lifestyles, bidding up

Despite a widely discussed oversupply of housing, Miami's residential marketplace appears to be bouncing back, with foreign investment providing a unique factor contributing to market resilience.

AP PHOTO/LYNNE SLADKY, FILE

"The ache for **home** lives in all of us, the safe place where we can go as we are and not be questioned."

—Maya Angelou

property prices—commercial and residential—well above other markets. That won't change.

But affordable workforce housing becomes an increasing challenge in gateway cities, which also harbor low-income communities and attract poor immigrants competing for service sector jobs. More people are in need of government housing assistance programs just as the government is shifting into austerity mode, resulting in a growing population of residents paying well over 30 percent of their incomes for housing. This limits what they can spend on all other aspects of life. As neighborhoods gentrify alongside prime areas, more poor people find themselves pushed into already deteriorating inner and outer rings where values will falter further, in step with degenerating housing and commercial stock. The decline and decay of entire neighborhoods, which used to be an exclusively "urban" problem, transforms into a dilemma for many more suburbs.

Connect

Of what value is

proximity?

connect

Of what value is **proximity?**

How is "location, location, location" being affected by ever new modes of communication? How are disruptive consumer preferences impacting real estate?

Technology Makes Some Places Less Important, Others More

As congestion and financial pressures push homes closer to jobs and shopping, the Internet allows us to operate from the fringe and beyond, sustaining demand for second homes in the country and resort locales. Proximity becomes more coveted, but not necessarily to the exclusion of distance. Somewhere between traditional proximity and Internet-enabled isolation, buildings get caught in a limbo of marginality and obsolescence. For more developers and owners, understanding and avoiding this twilight zone should take greater precedence.

Stiff-upper-lipped real estate players become less dismissive about what becomes more obvious: the information economy is revolutionizing communities and individuals alike. We can share work, meet with colleagues, make joint decisions, execute and return documents, and link to and from almost anywhere without any physical interaction with anyone. For much of what we do, operating from an office isn't as necessary as it once was. In fact, it's not necessary at all. And if we can wait a day or two for shipping, we can select, order, and obtain just about anything we need on the web without leaving home to traipse to a shopping center where we have to dodge conges-

What's next?

- Mobile Everything
- You Are Your Office
- Digital Asset Management
- Geo-coded Communications
- The Human Experience

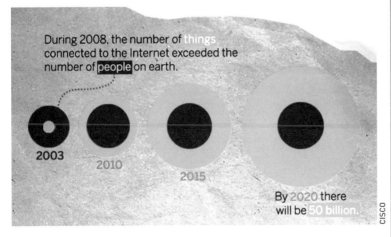

During 2008, the number of things connected to the Internet exceeded the number of people on earth.

2003

2010

2015

By 2020 there will be 50 billion.

CISCO

By 2020 there will be 50 billion things connected to the Internet. How will this change the way we live, work, and play?

tion and find parking. For many of us, the time we save by not traveling to a store on every whim more than makes up for the instant gratification of the purchase.

Whither the office and mall? Companies don't need as much space for employees and retailers don't need as many stores to reach their customers. Technology simply tempers the demand for commercial space—businesses can easily cut costs by leasing less square footage without any downside, and that expense savings fattens bottom lines—just not those of property owners.

The New Office: More Equals Less

The company headquarters or regional office transforms into more of a meeting place than a work space. Plenty of work gets done, but the office is more for intangibles and necessary face time—team and relationship building; bringing people together for important decisions, training, and development; and engaging clients or dealing directly with vendors. The new office environments need to promote interaction and dialogue, and be inviting for visitors. They must be flexible, to accommodate employees who spend less time there, while efficiently using space. Conference rooms, break areas, and open-office configurations take on increasing significance in layouts as tenants force down per employee space ratios.

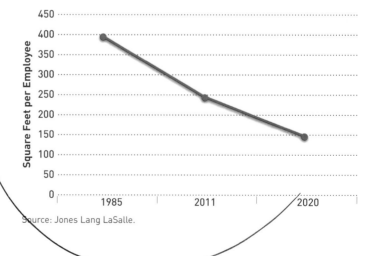

Average Space per U.S. Employee, All Industries

Source: Jones Lang LaSalle.

move common space needed

In high-tech and creative industries, cubicles are a thing of the past. High employee turnover among Gen Y is a great concern to tech-heavy tenants. Those landlords who can craft environments that attract and hold more young talent succeed. Google, Facebook, and Twitter all moved to more urban locations, seeking the stimulus-rich, urbane aura young people want. Young professionals sit in open areas where they can communicate freely with their co-workers to brainstorm. This can make the work experience more productive, energetic, and fun. Gen Y is a diverse, creative group that works well in teams and knows the value of

Facebook's headquarters in Palo Alto, California, has a modern, high-tech look and a fun atmosphere. Employees are encouraged to express themselves and make the space their own by writing on the walls, rearranging furniture, and adding artwork. The office includes impromptu work spaces, a DJ area, and numerous lounges.

CESAR RUBIO

collaboration, which is essential in today's global economy. Businesses that want to succeed over the next decade must harness the power of this generation by creating an office environment that appeals to them and sparks their creativity.

The Resilience of Centrality

Better technology doesn't negate the need for the in-person collaboration and competition that produces innovation and success. This is one reason major companies pay much more for space in a global gateway or 24-hour center and discount hard-to-get-to suburban places in order to retain and attract top talent. Google recently purchased one of the largest office buildings in Manhattan, a beaux arts building in central Paris, a historic warehouse in downtown Pittsburgh, and a property anchoring the pedestrian mall in Boulder. Companies pay to be close to knowledge, so as to reap the benefits of learning and collaboration. Biogen Inc. recently decided to leave its Weston, Connecticut, headquarters after only one year to return to Cambridge, Massachusetts. This will situate the company near Harvard University, MIT, and a quickly growing cluster of pharmaceutical companies.

Mobile versus Desktop Internet Users Worldwide, 2007–2015

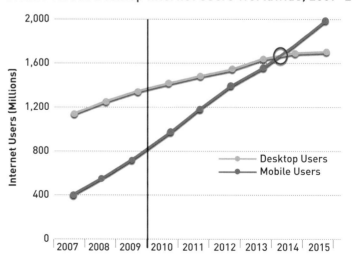

Source: Morgan Stanley Research.

Virtual Organizations

Small groups and partners can operate virtual companies effectively, linked together by computer devices and mobile phones from wherever they choose. If people know and trust each other, the need for face time diminishes, and they can always visit clients at their offices or get together with them at hotels. Bosses let staffers work more days from home— when kids are sick or when meetings aren't on the schedule. And bosses can extend their own weekends too, working from second homes or resort destinations on Fridays and Mondays. Of course, the broadband lines and mobile devices tether us to new job demands at a moment's notice, around the clock,

"The Hub," a co-working space in San Francisco.

HUB BAY AREA

wherever we are—that's the hitch to this new world order. Possibly the biggest downside for U.S. office demand comes from the global jobs arbitrage—the way that companies can operate in lower-cost global markets, connecting to well-educated personnel doing jobs at a fraction of U.S. wage and benefit rates.

Socialization versus Efficiency

Not everybody can or wants to work from home. Social interaction is essential for many of us. We need the office structure to get things done away from distractions, and we may just want to get out of the house for a change of scene. Co-working sites are becoming more common around the world for those who don't need to go to an office for these reasons. Nevertheless, the work-from-home option has obvious attractions—no commuting costs, more personal time, potentially greater productivity, and no dress codes—shorts, slippers, or just about whatever fits the bill. For the up-and-coming Gen Y crowd, multitasking, using virtual technology on the go, has become a way of life anyway. The right apps and the most adaptable devices—not where they sit and how they use those apps and devices—stir enthusiasm and enable productivity.

Do You Sleep with Your Cell Phone?—by U.S. Generation
Percentage who have ever placed their cell phone on or right next to their bed while sleeping.

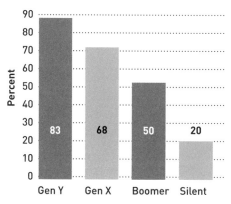

Source: Pew Research Center.

Home-Office Conversion

That erstwhile "den," "study," or "library" where pipe-smoking Dad in previous generations sought privacy and watched weekend golf tournaments on TV has become one of the most important rooms in the house for many prospective homebuyers. Maybe a converted attic or sun porch would work better. Apartment owners are hiring architects and brokers to reconfigure and market units to offer home-office amenities. Even studio apartments need room for a computer setup and desk space. Large multifamily residential properties may profit as much from adjacency to office supply stores as to supermarkets and cleaners.

Retail redux: Best Buy is slowing the growth of its big-box stores in favor of Best Buy Mobile locations, which focus on selling smartphones. These locations are only 3.6 percent of the square foot size of the traditional Best Buy.

RICHARD B. LEVINE

Connection Imperative

Keeping in the digital loop is necessary to keep a job. Resort and second-home developers would be wise to ensure that their accessory business centers offer best-in-class Internet access and wireless services. No matter where they find rest, business people looking to disengage from increasingly frenetic travel and meeting schedules will need to remain totally involved in handling organizational imperatives and communicating necessary directives or material information.

Gen Y and "Soft Programming"

Gen Yers, who grew up in the age of the Internet, lead the way in cell phone, Internet, and social media usage. Seventy-five percent of 18 to 29 year olds have a social networking profile. High technology use doesn't decrease the need for in-person communication; some would argue that it increases a person's social capital. Facebook users are shown to be more trusting, have more close relationships, and be more politically engaged than nonusers. Young people who flock to cities use technology to connect and engage with their community, essentially "using the Internet to get off the Internet." To target this generation, retailers and restaurants host networking, speed-dating, and

Registered Foursquare Users, March 2009–May 2011

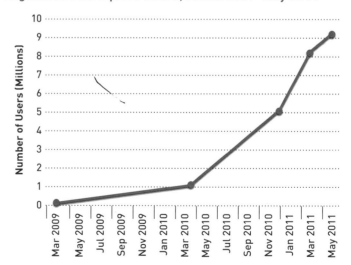

Source: Placepunch, 2011.

other events (all promoted on Facebook and Twitter) to entice young people to come out and meet each other. Older generations want this feeling of connectedness and community engagement as well. Downtown areas in cities and dense suburbs offer concerts, festivals, outdoor movies, and other events for families, young professionals, and people of all ages to enjoy and connect with their community.

The Shopping Scene: Integrating Place and Apps

At malls, logistics delivery technologies reduce the need for storage. Some types of stores disappear: books and recordings evaporate into the thin air of e-books and music apps. Fewer and fewer hardcovers, paperbacks, and DVDs get sold in physical space, and that goes for other goods, too. The formats of traditional department store anchors remain under siege, and the average chain store shrinks its displays. Merchandising strategies combine web and store marketing—retailers employ mobile apps and social networks to send messages about

Retail as experience: Apple patrons move freely about the store and loiter at the abundant number of stools and tables. Apple puts many units of each computer model on display and encourages patrons to use them.

BAT PHOTOS

location-based products and services, luring nearby customers to a point of purchase or using stores as pickup sites for e-purchases. The chains, operating from multiple formats, also can micro-target neighborhoods, depending on ethnic concentrations and local market needs, whether seasonal or event related. At the same time, more manufacturers discover how they can reach customers directly, cutting out retailers and wholesaler middlemen from transactions altogether.

Meeting Demand at the Right Place at the Right Time

Despite heightened virtual connection between people and places, we still get most of our stuff in traditional store formats, as we go shop in malls or urban districts that are most convenient, have the greatest selection, and offer the most entertaining distraction. Shopping center owners are joining forces with retailers to offer more community events—art shows, wine tastings, demonstrations, and speakers, anything that enables our need to see others and be seen. Run-of-the-mill or out-of-the-way malls without easy access get passed by and may be better suited to new forms of residential town center redevelopment.

More and more retail box formats are evolving into urban streetscape formats and gravitating to fortress malls and shopping centers at the heart of suburban nodes. Success in the shopping scene increasingly depends on integrating into other commercial and residential uses. The separation—disconnection—of land uses so prevalent in 20th-century suburban zoning gives way to an in situ community, even in the suburbs.

The new economy is rooted in virtual social networks that harness real locations at precise time periods to exercise prenegotiated variable-price transactions. New for the real estate industry? In its speed and volume only. But whether for hotel rooms, cars, bicycles, apartments, meeting space, food trucks, pop-up stores, cultural events or farmers markets, the temporary programming of real urban space grows ever more sophisticated. Want to draw more people into your storefront?

"We cannot live only for ourselves. A thousand fibers **connect** us with our fellow men."

—Herman Melville

Burnish the reputation of your building's address? Digital communications harness "geo-coded" information to deliver interactive messaging, creating new, location-specific advertising, advocacy, and community building. The real and virtual worlds collide as location-based advertising connects to a fleeting marketplace, enabling a new generation of urban place making and variable pricing strategies.

Renew

Where does your

energy come from?

Renew

Where does your **energy** come from?

In your city, business, home, or in yourself, where do you get the energy to thrive? Who will reap the value from managing your use of energy?

Recognizing the Need, Finding the Value

Green initiatives—like installing new-generation lighting or advanced building system controls, or buying smaller, more fuel-efficient cars—always get a boost when energy costs spike. But our fervor to conserve evaporates as soon as prices reverse and fall to easily affordable levels. For decades, plentiful energy has propelled a profitable inter-industry nexus of oil companies, automakers, real estate developers, homebuilders, and retail chains. Cheap and plentiful energy was the very foundation of America's consumer-based economy and 60 years of suburban development. No question, energy prices are going up.

Our ongoing "easy energy" habit leads to an opportunity for innovation. Our primary sources of abundant fuel are creating unintended consequences and prices remain volatile due to ever-growing global demand. We are reassessing where our energy will come from, but will demand and supply and regulatory frameworks align to create new markets? We are considering mobilizing capital to capture the value associated with

What's next?

- Energy Services Contracts
- Public Disclosure
- Demand Response Pricing
- Retrofitting and Repositioning
- Resilience to Disaster

Cost Savings of Energy Star–Labeled Buildings, 2010

Rank	Metropolitan Area	Number of Energy Star–Certified Buildings (2010)	Cost Savings ($ Millions)	Emissions Prevented (in Number of Homes' Worth of Electricity Use)
1	Los Angeles	510	117.9	39,800
2	Washington, DC	301	74.2	42,600
3	San Francisco	248	75.1	25,600
4	Chicago	232	62.7	54,500
5	New York	211	86.6	36,500
6	Atlanta	201	38.7	38,700
7	Houston	175	62.9	47,300
8	Sacramento	168	19.1	6,900
9	Detroit	151	18.7	17,400
10	Dallas–Fort Worth	148	35.2	26,300

Source: EPA.

the available resource of energy efficiency in buildings, but will creditworthiness and split market incentives allow us to invest?

With growing dependence on the Internet during an era of economic uncertainty, no business can afford to accept intermittent electricity delivery when power grids and network connections go down. As business leaders review risk mitigation strategies, more consider temporary or full-time onsite power generation capacity that avoids transmission networks. When it comes to transportation mobility and access to markets, higher driving costs may affect where companies decide to locate facilities and deploy personnel. As "nega-watts," "energy intensity," and "energy demand management" enter the real estate lexicon, these are no longer passing issues.

For the real estate industry, it's time to capture the value of the ubiquitous waste of energy throughout the economy. Buildings should be "spinning the meter in the opposite direction," and land use decision makers might be compelled to provide better, more cost-efficient locations. By doing so, property owners can meet tenants' demand for more value from each buck as more and more enterprises come under pressure to report on their sustainability performance as part of their bottom line.

Working the Competitive Edge

We're not talking about the future now. Recently completed and retrofitted Class A office projects are already securing market-leading rents and record prices, attracting tenants with energy-efficient designs that lower operating costs, enhance work environments, and create a halo for all parties involved. Under-floor building system technologies help produce healthier indoor climates through increased fresh air flow, natural convection, and individual workstation controls and decrease utility costs tied to heating and cooling air. Window and lighting technologies can adjust to daylight levels, reducing electricity bills while providing more comfortable work settings. No wonder tenants are gravitating to these projects—they build more enterprise value by occupying well-managed, efficient, green buildings.

Meeting Market Demand

Developers, owners, and investors are realizing that investing in available energy- and water-saving technologies can produce low-risk returns, creating more marketable and valuable real estate assets. Green roof designs and new building envelopes can help lower energy use—cooling by day and insulating at night. Onsite cogeneration plants can reduce building utility charges tied to peak demand, while providing tenants with power backup. More flexible interior designs can accommodate

Bank of America's New York skyscraper is the first skyscraper to receive LEED Platinum certification. It saves approximately 7.7 million gallons of water per year, and its onsite cogeneration system provides approximately 65 percent of the building's annual electricity requirements.

©COOK+FOX ARCHITECTS

movable wall options, enabling on-call reordering of workstation layouts—office configurations can be altered in hours, not days, without demolition expenses or employee dislocation. That enables the flexibility companies want as they lower per employee space requirements and use hoteling strategies to simultaneously increase the use intensity of office space.

Financing Retrofits

Owners can install energy-saving systems most economically as part of tenant improvement packages when leases roll over or when buildings are recapitalized. Core and shell makeovers significantly escalate costs and appear to be prohibitive, but office investors should consider the competitive implications of makeovers for attracting tenants and holding future value in buildings that come with yesterday's technologies and higher utility bills. Employers who want to attract high-potential

San Francisco's Public Utility Commission headquarters, to be completed in the summer of 2012, will include onsite treatment of gray and black water, saving approximately 750,000 gallons of water a year. It will also save $118 million in energy costs over the next 75 years.

©KMD ARCHITECTS

younger workers increasingly prefer high-performance, sustainable buildings, because Gen Yers harbor green priorities and favor working in more cutting-edge environments. Ignoring sustainability issues only speeds market obsolescence.

Leveraging Government's Push

The nation's largest portfolio owner, greatest energy consumer, and biggest office tenant—the U.S. government—is leading the charge to retrofit buildings to reduce its $25 billion annual energy bill by 28 percent by 2020 and thereby also reduce associated greenhouse gas emissions. Projects include solar power plants, advanced metering, roof upgrades, and water conservation initiatives. Cities and local governments across the country are also exploring a toolbox of carrots and sticks to coax building owners and tenants into power-saving practices. New York requires annual energy-efficiency benchmarking and energy system upgrades in the city's 24,000 largest buildings. Seattle set a goal for improving energy efficiency by 20 percent in existing buildings and 30 percent in new projects. Austin enacted code amendments for new single-family homes, requiring they produce as much energy as they consume. Chicago motivates building owners to install green roofs to help reduce heat island effects and electricity demand.

Average Area of New Single-Family Houses, United States

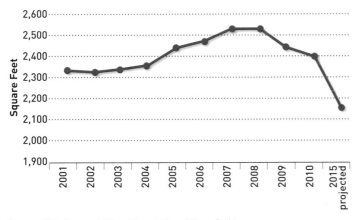

Sources: U.S. Census; National Association of Home Builders.

Compelling Cost Equations on the Home Front

As yo-yoing energy costs trend higher, households increasingly factor driving expenses (including fuel) and utility bills (heating and cooling big houses) into their calculations about where they want to live and work. If families can drop a car or two by moving closer to the office or near mass transportation, they can save not only at the pump but also on auto loans, insurance, and mainte-nance. One less car in a household means $100,000 or more in homebuying power. Time is money too—less time spent commut-ing or stuck in traffic doing errands can mean more profitable time at work or with family. This combination of convenience and savings impels changing lifestyle and housing preferences.

Compact Land Use Outcomes

Planners, builders, and investors can tap into this demand by adopting multifaceted, town-centric land use patterns, which provide greater housing and transportation choices for residents and reduce the number of vehicle miles traveled. Pedestrian-friendly neighborhoods around commercial centers (stores, restaurants, offices) with mid- and high-rise residenc-es make public transit more feasible and lower the household cost burdens for transportation. In these places, people can meet daily needs more economically, driving less and walk-ing or riding bikes more. Less driving helps relieve congestion and improve travel times, boosting overall system productiv-ity and mobility. Lower electric bills in smaller homes provide

U.S. Building Sector: Job Creation per $1 Billion of Spending

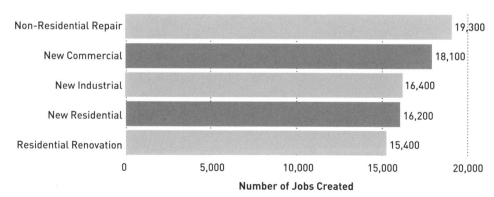

	Number of Jobs Created
Non-Residential Repair	19,300
New Commercial	18,100
New Industrial	16,400
New Residential	16,200
Residential Renovation	15,400

Source: Political Economy Research.

an added benefit, and reduced power usage and fewer vehicle miles traveled decrease pollution and carbon emissions.

Revitalizing Suburbs

A generation ago, cities struggled to implement inner-city urban renewal strategies. Now, the urban redevelopment challenge shifts to the suburbs, where an underutilized parking lot is a terrible thing to waste. Planners are refashioning abandoned shopping malls and reimagining failed retail strips, reviving subdivisions savaged in the foreclosure wave, and rethinking already entitled greenfield housing plans. In the future, depleted tax bases and declining support from federal and state coffers force more counties and towns to consolidate resources and consider regional solutions instead of cannibalistically competing for projects and new businesses.

Although plenty of bulldozing is in order, revamping and retooling existing buildings and spaces takes precedence over building new ones. As roads and sewage treatment plants reach the end of their life cycles, it's time to consider implementing smarter, more integrated solutions. And don't forget parks—as densifying suburbs lose more backyards, public recreation space becomes highly valued.

Average Annual U.S. Housing and Transportation Costs

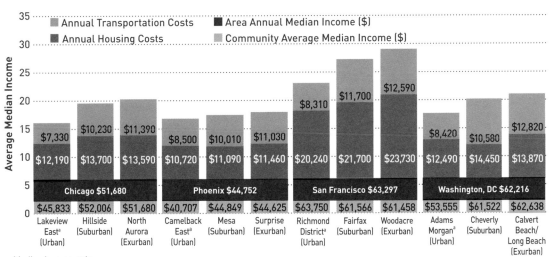

a. Median income only.
Source: CNT H+T Index.

Leveraging the Green

Manhattan's High Line park, built on top of an elevated railway trestle, drew 2 million visitors in 2010, created $2 billion in private investment on adjacent sites, and added 12,000 jobs in addition to the 8,000 construction jobs generated by building the park. Cities around the country are following Chicago's and New York's lead in transforming vacant rail or highway areas into beautiful parkland that spurs economic development. Philadelphia is considering turning the century-old Reading Viaduct into an elevated park, which it is believed will cost less than demolishing the structure. Downtown Birmingham transformed a vacant wasteland bounded by the railroad corridor into "Railroad Park." Dallas, Atlanta, and Seattle are in the midst of large-scale transformational green-space projects that will dramatically affect urban land use patterns.

Staying Hydrated

Ongoing stewardship of limited water resources has become a major concern for fast-growing states and cities across the parched Southwest and all communities that are dependent

Drought Conditions

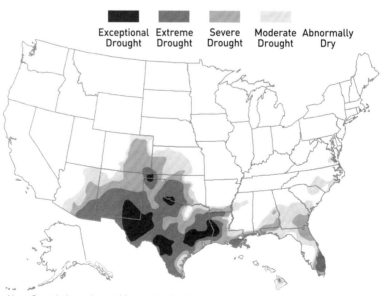

Note: Drought intensity as of 8 a.m., May 3, 2011.
Source: National Drought Mitigation Center.

> "Rest when you're weary. Refresh and **renew** yourself, your body, your mind, your spirit. Then get back to work."
>
> —Ralph Marston

on the Colorado River. Planners realize that these areas must reduce per capita water use and begin mandating water-reuse technologies in building projects as well as in communities. Without enough water, growth in these communities will simply stop. Developers need to get ahead of the curve by adopting water-saving plumbing and landscaping. In wetter areas where natural watershed and aquifer performance has been compromised, storm runoff pollution and flooding become major public policy issues. To limit damage, local governments have begun to enact new laws and fees that require more porous surfaces and retention systems.

Renewing Oneself, Renewing the Enterprise

The strategic role that real estate plays in renewing communities won't be lost on the real estate enterprise itself. As the industry's collective trauma from the financial crisis burns off into a series of new market opportunities, individuals and corporate teams seek to renew themselves, their strategies, and all of the assumptions in their business plans. Business practices become ever more community and user-oriented. Emphasis on leadership and positive community engagement is sustained by professional development retreats and mid-career educational tune-ups. Renewing in real time becomes a necessary component of professional life, as more participation in online communities enriches both personal productivity and enterprise value.

Where do you want to go?

How will transportation infrastructure define market value? How will innovation be cultivated within local communities?

Adjusting Where We Go and How We Choose to Get There

Certainly, the housing crisis has slowed our urge to relocate. Many homeowners with underwater mortgages simply find themselves stuck. Stricter lending standards suddenly make trading up much harder and less affordable. So scratch the dream home in a nicer community for now. Prospective buyer confidence is sagging. Will home values ratchet up again? Can the jobs scene improve dramatically enough to lift prices? Without a better job or a big raise, the opportunity to move is less likely, unless we're downsizing. Many of us simply resign ourselves to stay put for a while.

"Being There"

Strained finances also put a premium on reducing transportation costs—particularly car-related expenses—and traveling shorter distances. Looking ahead, more Americans want to live in places closer to shopping districts and mass transit lines to get to work. Walking to the supermarket has newfound cachet. As businesses that are isolated in office parks or in fringe districts encounter increasing trouble attracting high-quality work forces, more companies look for central locations. Developers

What's next?

- Move to Work
- Bus Rapid Transit
- More Walking; Less Parking
- Vehicle Sharing
- 360-Degree Port Logistics

Movers Who Moved Out of State, 2001/02–2009/10

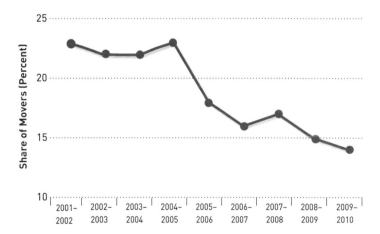

Source: U.S. Census 2010.

almost cannot go wrong with well-conceived transit-oriented projects. The back-to-the-future notion of building housing in and around commercial districts gets a boost.

Job-Driven Relocation

The ongoing fiscal crunch shouldn't stop growing numbers of highly educated Gen Yers, unfettered by mortgages and major family responsibilities, from moving at a moment's notice for a solid job offer or anything to boost nascent career prospects. But those opportunities are more likely to stem from employers in global gateways and 24-hour centers that already feature compact development and mass transit alternatives. Mostly 20-something singles find their less-encumbered lifestyles well suited to urban infill convenience. This cohort's percentage of miles driven, car ownership, and possession of a driver's license already ranks below other age groups. Car-sharing services will multiply across large urban centers and college towns, offering new web-enabled alternatives to sharing vehicles across communities.

North American Car-Sharing Members

Source: Shaheen & Cohen, 2010; Carsharing.net.

Will Weather-Related Risk Influence Location Decisions?

Over the past 50 years, hurricanes haven't deterred a population explosion concentrated along Florida's coasts. California has rapidly emerged as the nation's most populous state despite a looming threat from "The Big One." Remember, Naples still sits proudly at the base of Mount Vesuvius. Water shortages, storm events, and heat waves force communities to adapt; many are already deeply engaged in reassessing levies and flood maps. But can we bank on federal and state governments to continue to subsidize insurance frameworks and help rebuild communities whenever disaster strikes? As politicians slash spending and revisit governance philosophies, those dollars may not be available. Communities and geographic regions could become either more expensive or less desirable.

Seniors and Convenience

The Boomers, the other large demographic group, embrace pedestrian-friendly places as they move into the 65-plus age range. Accessibility to grocery stores and doctors' offices informs housing decisions, and a majority favor communities where walking is easy and safe. For many, access to mass transit is especially critical for getting around on a highly constrained budget. Seniors made 328 million more trips using public transit in 2009 than in 2001, and this number will surely

Trips by U.S. Seniors on Public Transit, 2001–2009

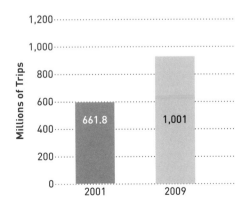

Source: Transportation for America.

rise as their population grows. More developers of senior and independent housing communities should take note—residences near hospital centers and medical offices will be popular, especially if integrated into mixed-use neighborhoods with plenty of nearby shops, restaurants, and services.

Unclogging Arteries

Too many cars and trucks on highways that are unable to handle ever-increasing volumes inflict time-wasting costs and productivity declines, exacerbated by expected population gains in the nation's important gateways. New airports and tracking systems are needed to help alleviate overcrowded flight paths, and outmoded rail systems are insufficient to meet rising demand. The United States is home to five of the world's ten busiest airports and has embedded aviation mobility as a way of life. Taxpayers and users reluctantly will confront paying more to rebuild and expand already burdened infrastructure to overcome obsolescence and congestion-related problems. Although investing in transport systems hasn't been a recent priority in Washington, if states and cities do not come around to it, these networks will become less reliable and more dangerous, and will limit economic growth. Regional planners need to attempt to integrate multimodal infrastructure initiatives—including mass transit alternatives—into future land use schemes, helping connect evolving suburban centers, metropolitan cores, and transportation hubs. These networks will take decades to build out, but the time to start is now.

Homebuyers' Responses: Best Long-Term Solutions to Congestion

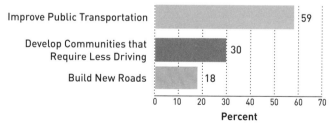

Source: National Association of Realtors, 2011.

Taking a Long-Term View

Any new transportation investment needs to produce corresponding land use outcomes, such as the redevelopment of suburban nodes into more mixed-use, higher-density, residential-retail-office districts. Over time, well-planned regional networks can connect these expanding centers and link to downtown cores, airports, and other mass transportation systems.

The Transbay Transit Center in San Francisco plans to accommodate more than 100,000 passengers each weekday through multiple modes of transit. It will create a new transit-friendly neighborhood with 3,400 new homes and mixed-use commercial development.

PELLI CLARKE PELLI ARCHITECTS, SINGER ASSOCIATES INC.

Bringing in the Private Capital (Strategically)

Local governments should partner with private investors to finance new projects. Many of the country's original subway and trolley systems were built by private companies allied with land developers and local governments. Why shouldn't this model work again in updated approaches? Missteps can be avoided by sharing risks and rewards appropriately between private operators, governments, users, and taxpayers. A National Infrastructure Bank, modeled on Europe's successful investment bank (the European Investment Bank), could finance economically sensible, merit-based projects and attract private capital through sound financial underwriting. U.S. pension funds and insurance companies are now investing 1 to 2 percent of assets in infrastructure funds, much of it in international projects. Why not in U.S. projects? Many believe that these institutional investors may grow their holdings in such funds to 4 to 5 percent of assets. Local authorities and developers can capture some of these investments for well-conceived, integrated projects, while making an important improvement in quality of life for the very people who invested the funds in the first place.

Paying Attention to Rails, Airports, and Ports

While improving national mobility, government and industry need to work with planners to streamline supply chains and

The planned Washington Metro Silver Line will offer a viable alternative to vehicular traffic to Dulles airport and support future transit-oriented development along the Dulles corridor. This transportation improvement will double the number of jobs in office buildings, multiplying the number of residents more than five times without appreciably increasing traffic congestion.

FAIRFAX COUNTY, VIRGINIA

invest in intermodal connections, which link to the global economy. Among the desperately needed items on the wish list, expanding ports must be seamlessly served by upland collection and distribution links—ideally designed to expand both local and regional economies. The nation's primary ocean ports require new rail lines to speed goods outside harbor districts and decrease traffic on local interstates, which are gridlocked by truck congestion. A national strategy for moving goods efficiently back and forth from strategic ports and regional commercial centers across the country is a priority.

And we shouldn't forget about advancing air transportation. Skyrocketing flight delays could be ameliorated around gateway air hubs if we replaced World War II radar technologies for tracking jets with state-of-the-art navigation systems. Spacing between jets can be shortened and weather-related delays reduced.

Getting Fit: More Walking and Biking

Only a tiny fraction, under half a percent, of Americans bike to work, but some cities find that bike lanes and bike-sharing programs can boost bike commuting. Pedestrian and bike improvements have been documented to improve local retail

Expanding Transit Markets

Boston
Denver
Detroit
Honolulu
Houston
Los Angeles
Minneapolis
New York
Portland
Salt Lake City
San Francisco
Seattle
Washington, DC

Source: ULI analysis of various sources.

U.S. Fuel-Economy Standards for Cars and Light Trucks

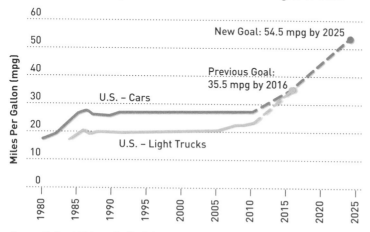

New Goal: 54.5 mpg by 2025

Previous Goal: 35.5 mpg by 2016

U.S. – Cars

U.S. – Light Trucks

Miles Per Gallon (mpg)

Source: National Highway Traffic Safety Administration.

performance on a block by block basis. On the high end, 6 percent of people in Portland, Oregon, bike to work; 4 percent in Minneapolis; and more than 2 percent in San Francisco and Washington, D.C. Studies show that, on average, urban dwellers walk and bike more and have lower levels of obesity and weight-related health problems than car-bound suburbanites. Bike sharing is proliferating across urban communities. Many office building owners, prompted by tenants and Leadership in Energy and Environmental Design (LEED) standards, are considering providing bike storage and shower facilities for workers. In turn, more workers may start pedaling.

Federal and local governments explore incentives to promote adoption of electrical vehicles. The city of Portland and many other state and municipal governments are seeking to make the transition from demonstration projects to broader market adoption of electric vehicles and associated charging stations.

AP PHOTO/RICK BOWMER

"All mankind is divided into three classes: those that are immovable, those that are movable, and those that **move**."

—Benjamin Franklin

Where Is the Electric Car?

With higher government standards for fuel efficiency in the pipeline and concerns over climate change growing, the push by carmakers to increase production of electric cars and hybrids should start developers and building owners thinking about future-proofing their parking garages. The owners and dreamers of electric cars prompt officials to rewrite building codes to require plug-in fixtures in parking garages, as some European governments already do. Look to tenant demand to drive investments in retrofitting buildings with charging stations, and look to corporate vehicle fleets as early innovators in large-scale deployment.

Invest

Where will **growth, value,**

and **risk** come from?

Invest

Where will **growth, value,** and **risk** come from?

How will real estate be financed? What will private equity demand?

Global Capital Tapping Local Assets

Make no mistake—the way we invest and think about real estate assets has changed radically over the past two decades. The notion of patient money, getting rich slowly, husbanding cash flows, and nurturing tenant relationships with hands-on management has given way. Properties and communities are growing more disconnected from investors and lenders. Often, the ownership group of that office or apartment building lives in a different time zone, if not a different country.

Today, residential finance in the United States is virtually all federally backed, except for a small amount of portfolio lending for those with the very best credit. And no one knows what will happen to or what new form will be shaped for Fannie and Freddie. As to the structure of the residential mortgage-backed security market, that is still up in the air, with the federal role wide open and the Dodd-Frank rules not yet established. Welcome to the next decade of financial governance reform.

Who buys with the intent to hold any more? And who goes into an investment for single-digit returns? Not many of us. Wall Street bankers and institutional managers have transformed essentially illiquid real estate into a cyclical trading instrument with a capital stack configuration of investment options more akin to stocks and bonds. Angling for the highest possible risk-adjusted yields, they funnel money relentlessly from global channels into various funds and investment wrappers. And this imperfect process—sort of like fitting a square peg into a round hole—remains intact despite the recent crash.

If anything, future real estate markets become more globalized and interconnected, with capital coursing across regions and through different channels. Countries continue to establish real estate investment trust (REIT) markets. Portfolios expand, with internationally diversified holdings becoming the norm. More governments allow commercial mortgage–backed security (CMBS) financing; debt securities already provide up to 40 percent of European finance and 33 percent of Asia Pacific finance. Undoubtedly, investment banks must increase operations to marry capital to product across continents and oceans.

What's next?

- Regulatory Reform
- Global Capital
- More Securitization
- More REITs
- Risk Transparency

The profitable "trading and finance" genie is out of the bottle, whether real estate can be easily commoditized or not, and players around the world remain starved for yield and need ready sources of funding.

Today, capital sources and investment committees make buy-sell and lending decisions without firsthand market knowledge of complicated local fundamentals, let alone site visits. Operating from far-off places, they often depend on reams of advisor-consultant recommendations, analyst studies, and credit rating reports.

In the new trading dynamic, these disconnected investors can pay little mind to how buy or sell decisions affect the future of assets beyond temporary holding periods, let alone the micro effects of sell decisions or workouts on places in which these properties are located. Results-driven limited partners and plan sponsors concentrate their attention in document reviews on internal rates of return and how long it takes to score anticipated returns, while general partners or investment managers

Contribution to GDP and GDP Growth by Type of City

■ Developed economies   ▨ Emerging-market middleweight cities
■ Emerging-market megacities   ▨ Emerging-market small cities and rural areas

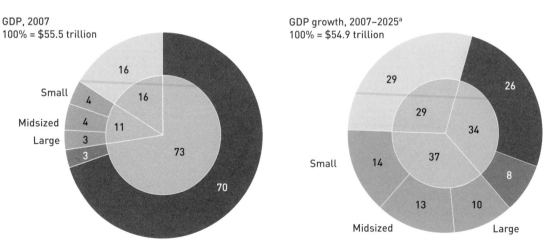

GDP, 2007
100% = $55.5 trillion

GDP growth, 2007–2025[a]
100% = $54.9 trillion

Notes: Megacities = metropolitan areas with 10 million or more inhabitants. Middleweights = 150,000 to 10 million inhabitants.
a. Real exchange rate (RER) for 2007 is the market exchange rate. RER for 2025 was predicted from differences in the per capita GDP growth rates of countries relative to the United States.
Source: McKinsey Global Institute Cityscope 1.0.

look ahead to reinvesting proceeds in follow-on offerings as long as the cycle allows. And at some point a next-generation fund will miss the market turn, resulting in big losses. Can you blame advisors or general partners? Their business model just doesn't work if they sell down client assets and stop investing, and private equity real estate doesn't allow quick exits, even with capital stacks.

How does this cycle play out? Almost inevitably, the left-for-dead CMBS market rebounds, and ample money returns to debt and equity plays from myriad domestic and overseas sources, looking for opportunity in the new cycle. Though somewhat sedated from recent loss shocks, investment libidos still crave less greedy but generous mid-teens returns in recovery even though a reversion to the mean seems more plausible and reasonable for the longer term. Not coincidentally, many intermediaries continue to market investment funds with built-in promotes and lucrative transaction fees, designed to secure shorter-term value spikes over long-term cash flow performance. It's just hard to be satisfied with less.

But Less May Be More

Less may be more, especially if we consider the short list of hard lessons learned and relearned from our recent industry debacle, when capital momentum too easily lost track

U.S. CMBS Issuance

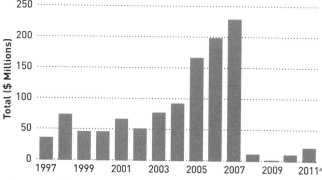

a. Issuance total through August 30, 2011.
Source: Commercial Mortgage Alert.

of market supply and demand trends. Top tips for the future resemble good lessons from the past:

1. Watch economic trends, especially employment and wage moves. Jobs drive real estate demand, and anemic jobs growth—or worse, decline—spells trouble.

2. For investors, project viability and profitability relate well to local and regional economic growth trends, not just individual project forecasts.

3. Diversification doesn't protect against the systemic risk of global credit market breakdown or losses from blindly buying pools of inferior assets.

4. The availability of voluminous public information about loans and underlying properties in securities offerings doesn't mean analysts, including credit rating agencies, can or will adequately digest and produce meaningful guidance for enlightened decision making.

5. It's hard to hedge illiquid, often cyclical assets; highly touted financial engineering strategies didn't work. All that market liquidity from multiple sources can dramatically pump up demand—or shut off just as suddenly, potentially creating more market volatility, not less.

U.S. Commercial and Multifamily Mortgage Maturities

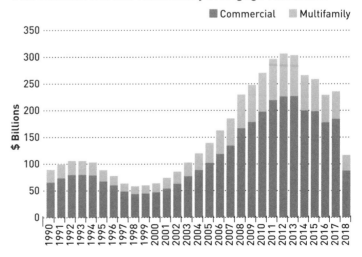

Sources: Federal Reserve Board, Foresight Analytics LLC.

"Only **buy** something that you'd be perfectly happy to hold if the market shut down for ten years."

—Warren Buffett

6. The essential difference between core, value add, and opportunistic risk-return strategies (outside of development) relates to the amount of leverage put on investments, and leverage used late in any cycle can be extremely dicey and can make performance implode.

7. The dynamic impact of technology is transforming how and where tenants use space. Every economic sector faces significant change. We're in a new era when properties can turn obsolete faster.

8. Embrace the 7 to 10 percent annualized returns that real estate can dependably deliver. Early in a cycle, intrepid investors and developers can make more, but the window of opportunity closes quickly as soon as mainstream capital follows on.

9. Invest in people. Encourage everyone in your company to get smarter about energy, sustainability, transportation, and communications, so you can anticipate change and deal with it profitably.

10. Keep an eye on what's happening in global markets. In a globalizing economy, we can find great ideas outside the United States, and profits increasingly depend on serving overseas markets better.

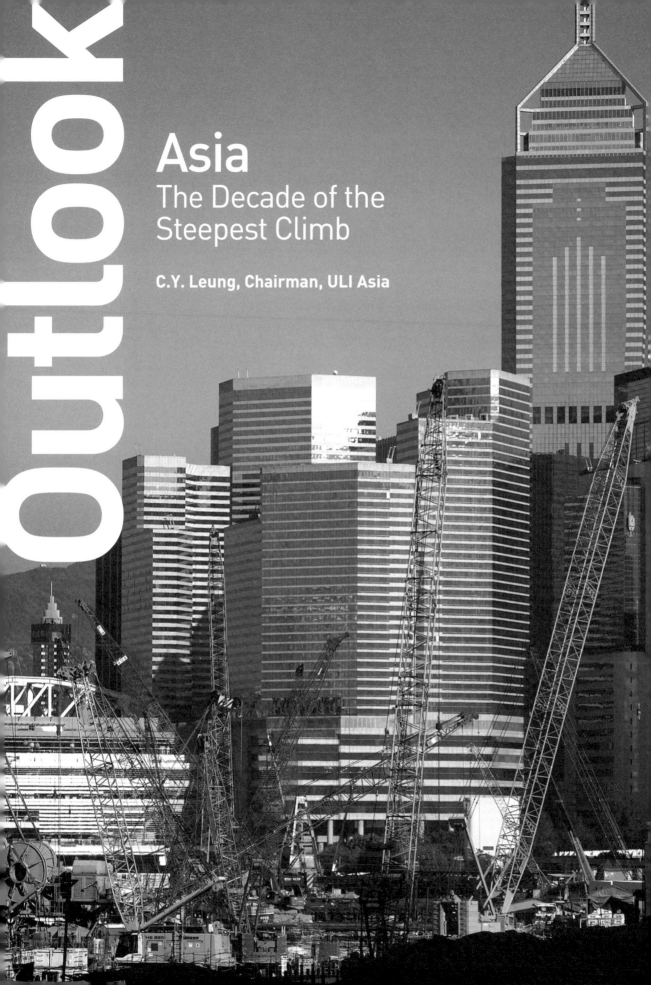

Outlook

Asia
The Decade of the
Steepest Climb

C.Y. Leung, Chairman, ULI Asia

As ULI celebrates its 75th anniversary of pursuing "the responsible use of land," Asia faces a decade that will mark the apex of changes in land use and human settlements in the broader context of a century of change between 1950 and 2050. Nearly all Asian countries are going through a radical transformation, most notably Indonesia, India, and China. Together these three domestic markets represent well over half of the world's population.

Understanding the ways that rapid urbanization contributes to driving economic activity and the creation of social equity is a core theme of ULI conversations in Asia. Many believe that, in fact, the next decade of Asian urbanization will drive the global economy. The growing concentration of domestic populations in urban communities means that construction activities associated with infrastructure, combined with new development in the property sector, translate into an urban-driven economic equation. We see this theme picked up by "smart city" marketing campaigns and in

What does unprecedented urban development look like?

From country to city, how will swelling urban populations learn to thrive? How will invented cities and cities that are millennia old form the basis for a new global economy?

National Urbanization Rates, 2010

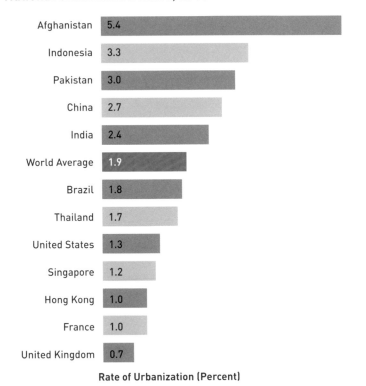

Afghanistan	5.4
Indonesia	3.3
Pakistan	3.0
China	2.7
India	2.4
World Average	1.9
Brazil	1.8
Thailand	1.7
United States	1.3
Singapore	1.2
Hong Kong	1.0
France	1.0
United Kingdom	0.7

Rate of Urbanization (Percent)

Source: *CIA Factbook*, 2011.

the growing internationalization of global capital participating in the real estate and infrastructure sectors.

In fact, the real story of the coming decade in Asia—behind the headlines of the cranes, the shiny trains, and the new buildings—is the maturation of the capital markets. There'll be no new delivery of buildings and infrastructure without well-functioning money markets. To put a face on this coming transformation, let's take a look at projected volume of construction.

Dimensions of Growth

By 2020, construction in Asia Pacific doubles, fueling growth for all of the construction industry. According to PwC, global construction activities are projected to expand by 70 percent, from $7 trillion to $12 trillion in just nine years. Three domestic economies around the world— the United States, China, and India—represent over 50 percent of that growth between 2011 and 2020, accounting for $5 trillion. A total of 45 domestic markets represent 85 percent of global construction activity by 2020. The opportunities for collaboration around best practices in urban investment, real estate development, and infrastructure delivery are clear.

Housing will be the largest global subsector, while infrastructure is expected to show the fastest rate of growth. In infrastructure, global sports events and nuclear and renewable energy help drive demand, on top of a broad array of projects dealing with the environment.

A Network of Chinese Cities

By 2020, in China alone, 400 cities will have populations over 1 million, compared with 40 cities in the United States. In the past decade, Shanghai, Beijing, and Hong Kong have become globally recognized cities, taking center stage at the 2008 Olympic

Games and in the recent Shanghai World Fair and Expo. Many market watchers may now recognize the strategic growth of Shenzhen, Tianjin, and Wuhan. Now get ready for the 394 other cities in China. As market networks mature, look to secondary

Urban China

Sources: Population Division of the Department of Economic and Social Affairs of the United Nations Secretariat, *World Population Prospects: The 2008 Revision* and *World Urbanization Prospects: The 2009 Revision*, http://esa.un.org/wup2009/unup/.

and tertiary cities to grow rapidly as niche flows of capital seek efficiency in supply chains and dramatic gains in productivity.

China's larger cities, with populations greater than 2.5 million, continue to be of strong interest to real estate investors who are active in the region. ULI's recent survey of Chinese cities indicates that real estate investors express preferences for Chengdu, Shanghai, Chongqing, and Beijing. However, the remaining cities in the ULI survey—Nanjing, Wuhan, Dalian, Qingdao, Tianjin, Wuxi, Shenzhen, Suzhou, Hangzhou, Guangzhou, Changsha, and Shenyang—are all favorably rated as having strong prospects for investment return.

Evolving Investor Appeal

Overall, ULI Asia members believe that at least 16 markets in China are of strong interest, emphasizing the extraordinary appeal of Asian markets as a place to invest and develop. The explosive growth of these cities, with eight of these markets having populations over 5 million, is result-

Emerging-Market Cities' Growing Role in Global Economy

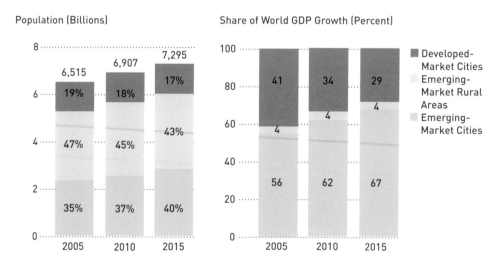

Note: Rural GDP is the agricultural portion of GDP; city GDP is nonagricultural GDP. Some numbers do not add to 100 because of rounding.

Sources: Boston Consulting Group analysis of United Nations, *World Urbanization Prospects: The 2009 Revision;* Economist Intelligence Unit; BCG analysis.

ing in a wave of urban development that is difficult for many outside China to comprehend.

The sheer quantity of urban investment is driving the creation of a new generation of professional practices in all aspects of investment, design, development, and management of properties. Recently, a ULI member in Shanghai noted, "It is an accepted fact that Western global real estate firms are behind their direct competitors in Asia, both their competitors in Asia Pacific and domestic Chinese, by almost one full wave."

The wholesale creation of new communities is driving demand across all real estate product types. Retail and industrial properties lead the way, while multifamily residential, hospitality, and

In 2010 alone, visitor arrivals to Asia exceeded 200 million, a 13 percent increase from the number of visitors in 2009.

office properties are all strong. The massive investment in a new high-speed rail network is fostering new paradigms of mixed-use transit-oriented development, especially in city centers. An emerging leisure industry, fueled by rapidly growing domestic tourism, is driving a range of experimentation in new place-making strategies at resort and heritage tourism destinations.

Within an industry characterized as "always local," China's markets stand out as among the most localized in the world. Each city represents its own investment environment, many of them not necessarily tied to national policy or aggregate economic trends. Local laws, regulations, and implementation capacity play as large a role in shaping the urban investment and development climate as the directives issued by the central government provide an underlying framework.

Niche or emerging market opportunities are driven by changing demographics and the enormous growth of the middle class. With China's senior population soaring, resorts and senior housing are in great demand; and business park development—a land use typology that is just now beginning to mature—has been spurred by the surge in auto use.

Rising Middle Class

By 2020, Asia's rising middle class is projected to reach an amazing 1.7 billion. According to the Organization for Economic Co-operation and Development, that represents over half of the coming global middle-class population. This translates into a series of new Asian economies filled with households with real discretionary budgets making real choices about where they want to live, shop, and spend recreational time. Already, there's much speculation regarding what you'll find in their shopping bags or where they'll want to spend their holidays. As incomes rise and tastes mature, Asia's consumers are dramatically drawn to global luxury brands, and the aspirations of the middle class across all Asian markets are a powerful catalyst for the creation of high-quality retail and leisure environments.

The widely reported uptrend in luxury retail, coupled with rising tourism flows, will accelerate the evolution of Asian models of mixed-use retail formats, particularly in those markets with unbearable summer humidity. Fly to Hong Kong or Beijing to shop for the weekend? How about to Wuhan? McKinsey has already projected that by 2015 China will represent the world's largest luxury market. The regional and urban development dimensions of this wave of consumer spending have not been fully appreciated. It raises questions like, will existing Asian gateway cities capture all of this growth and distinguish their real estate markets over the long term? Will the combined impact of better airports and the emerging growth of online retailing distribute the creation of high-quality retail environments over many cities? And what about Asian demand in international markets? Will the traditional European and U.S. retail markets benefit dramatically?

Tourism, especially domestic tourism, represents a core driver of revenue for select Asian cities, and the potential driver for the diversification of the resort and hospitality sectors. Consumer confidence has steadily been on the rise, although temporary events such as the Japanese earthquake and the Indonesian tsunami do have broader impacts on the industry. The Nielsen Asia-Pacific Consumer Confidence Index, a measure of overall willingness on behalf of Asian consumers to spend, rose to a new height in spring 2011. On a global basis, seven of the top ten domestic markets with the most optimistic consumers lie in countries in Asia Pacific.

Retail spending across Asian markets is boosted by strong international visitor arrivals. In 2010 alone, visitor arrivals to the region exceeded 200 million. Swelling at 13 percent year over year, this double-digit growth rate is expected to continue over the next decade. The United Nations World Tourism Organization ranks select Asian destinations in the top global tourist destinations, and we can expect their numbers to grow as the world explores the millennia-old cultural traditions of Asia.

Growth Challenges

Yet with respect to ecology and environment, the economic vibrancy and heady growth faces some growing headwinds. Asia's long-term future is seriously threatened by a growing water crisis in many regions. Per capita, fresh water availability in the Asian region is among the lowest in the world. Intense competition is emerging between cities for shared water resources. Health risks continue to rise as many cities suffer from air pollution and recklessly discard untreated human and hazardous wastes into freshwater bodies. An integrated approach to urban water management is essential for the social, economic, and environmental sustainability of cities. As the structure of economies changes, Asia, like many Western cities, needs to learn how to recycle urban land by recovering contaminated brownfield sites left behind by 20th-century industries. The speed and unprecedented nature of community development in Asia creates ample challenges to the real estate and city building industries to sustain thriving communities through the responsible use of land.

Advice to Market Participants

ULI members in Asia recently distilled advice to market participants seeking to enter Asian markets:

- Do your best. You're only as good as your last project. Emphasis on quality and reputation is paramount.

- New capital flowing into the real estate sector doesn't mean that prevailing knowledge and expertise is aligned with the expectations of government gatekeepers. Projects seeking to innovate on past practices and chart new directions for the marketplace must also navigate the trends and realities of the public approvals process.

- Markets are dynamic and major investments are ongoing—the urban context is in many instances an urban planning context. The building across the street may be there only for another two to three years before it's replaced. The same goes for infrastructure. Know the plan.

ULI clearly has a unique role to play in fostering an unprecedented collection of urban development best practices in Asia. To be a global organization and to fulfill its mission, ULI must have a strong presence in Asia. The opportunity to assist with challenges presented by the region's rapid urbanization, the potential of significant growth in membership and influence for the Institute, and the committed support of ULI's Asia leadership all combine to make it the right time for ULI's investment in Asia.

Outlook

Europe

Gareth Evans, Inside Cities

The global financial crisis has fundamentally altered the economic landscape throughout Europe. Before the crisis, the European Union (EU) was characterized by the most intense period of economic expansion and integration in the postwar era. The 1993 Treaty of Maastricht built the foundation for this integration. Since 1993, the EU has grown steadily from its 12 founding member states to 27, through two rounds of expansion in 1995 and 2004.

Over the last ten years especially, the rate of economic growth within the EU has been rapid. The single market has increased trade in the EU by 150 percent since its creation, and the total stock of foreign direct investment in the EU, attracted primarily by the prospects offered by such a huge single market, stood at $5.4 trillion as the global financial crisis broke in 2007. The impact of the global financial crisis, however, has been palpable. Europe and its cities must reevaluate and reassess their inherent strengths and weaknesses, while identifying and seeking to take advantage of new economic opportunities presented by the crisis.

In order to take full advantage of these opportunities and to ensure that Europe stays ahead of its competitors, ULI Europe proposes that Europe and its cities adopt six fundamental principles:

1. Live in sustainable housing in a mixed market.

2. Work in growing new industries, as well as traditional strengths.

3. Invest in new assets that are globally competitive.

4. Connect with growth opportunity.

5. Engage with Europe's neighbors to increase scale and opportunity.

6. Lead the world in energy efficiency and sustainable development.

The Impact of the Crisis

The global financial crisis halted Europe's sustained period of rapid economic growth, expansion, and integration, uncovering some fundamental structural weaknesses within the EU's

Europe is a continent, depending on how one defines it, of up to 500 million people, many of whom are only recently emerging into a world of free economic trade and movement. We see important opportunities in both mature and emerging parts of Europe but no shortage of challenges. ULI's role in this context is to support members, organizations, and cities across Europe to redefine their positions within the global real estate and economic marketplace.

—JOE MONTGOMERY, CEO, ULI EUROPE

institutional arrangements. It has forced the EU to reevaluate its economic gains and pushed the EU's member states collectively into a new epoch, characterized by medium- to long-term uncertainty and slow economic growth.

Sovereign Debt and the Single Currency

The global financial crisis has created concerns regarding the future of the euro. When the euro was launched, it was hoped that increased trade and investment between eurozone nations would lead to a truly unified European economy. The financial crisis, however, has highlighted the lack of political union between eurozone states, as well as member countries' inability to adjust to an asymmetric shock, and its deflationary impact, through domestic fiscal policy and exchange rate adjustments.

This concern is being compounded by worries over Europe's growing sovereign debt problem, which began to emerge in late 2009. Although the crisis has affected members of the EU to varying degrees—most notably Greece, Spain, Ireland, Italy, and Portugal—rising sovereign debt has become a perceived problem for Europe as a whole. Subsequent concern about rising government deficits and debt levels on a global scale, as well as a swath of moves to downgrade European government debt, has created a period of grave uncertainty in global financial markets.

The EU responded on May 9, 2010, as all 27 member states agreed to create the European Financial Stability Facility (EFSF), a legal instrument designed to preserve Europe's financial stability by providing financial assistance worth €750 billion to those EU states in difficulty. The EFSF has gone some way to helping to restore global financial markets' confidence in Europe, but future stability still looks uncertain at this point, especially in countries such as Greece where the sovereign debt problem is threatening to spiral out of control and devaluation seems inevitable.

Unemployment

The financial crisis has had a hugely adverse affect on unemployment rates throughout the 27 EU member states. The impact of the economic crisis between 2008 and 2010 completely wiped out the reduction experienced in the unemployment rate between 2004 and 2008. The unemployment rate rose from 7.2 percent in March 2008 to 9.5 percent in May 2009 in the eurozone, while the rate in the EU increased from 6.7 percent to 8.9 percent. The overall unemployment rate in the 27 EU member states reached 9.7 percent in July 2010.

Although unemployment rates are of huge concern to individual member state governments, as well as the EU as a whole, it is the longevity of this unemployment that has the potential to affect Europe's economy most adversely. In 2010, 3.8 percent of the EU's labor force had been unemployed for more than one year. While job losses have been contained for some time by flexible unemployment benefit arrangements, eventually the impact of long-term unemployment will be felt by governments. Long-term unemployment often leads to a permanent loss of skills, as well as extra pressure on the fiscal positions of governments as their long-term tax base shrinks, hindering city competitiveness as well as compounding the sovereign debt crisis.

Le Grand Paris is an ambitious urban regeneration project started by French President Nicolas Sarkozy. The project aims to improve connectivity among the eight counties in Paris's metropolitan region by updating transport infrastructure.

LE GRAND PARI DE L'AGGLOMÉRATION PARISIENNE

The Investment Environment

The global financial crisis was preceded by a long period of rapid credit growth, low risk premiums, abundant availability of liquidity, strong leveraging, increasing asset prices, and the development of bubbles in the real estate sector. Overstretched leveraging positions rendered financial institutions extremely vulnerable to corrections in asset markets.

In its early stages, the crisis manifested itself as an acute liquidity shortage among financial institutions. When Lehman Brothers defaulted in September 2008, however, confidence collapsed, investors liquidated their positions, and stock markets crashed. The speed of the transmission of financial distress to the real economy in the EU was unprecedented, with credit restraint and falling confidence discouraging business investment and household demand, notably for consumer durables and housing.

The European economy as a whole turned from one based on rapid growth, facilitated by access to relatively cheap credit, to a much more conservative investment environment. As credit has become increasingly scarce, companies have been forced to scale back their investment activities across a wide variety of sectors, most notably in real estate and research and development.

Adjusting to New Norms and the Road Ahead

The global financial crisis has forced Europe's cities to rethink and alter their future development strategies to adjust to new economic and social norms. While individual countries and cities will pursue a path of development that takes into account their own inherent strengths and weaknesses, there must also be a collective and unified response across Europe, something which is reflected in the European Commission's Europe 2020 Strategy. Europe's ability to adjust to the new economic and social norms that the global financial crisis has created will ultimately decide its collective success over the next decade. ULI Europe proposes that there are six fundamental principles that Europe's cities, as well as Europe as a collective unit, must adopt if they are to truly turn crisis into opportunity.

1. Live in Sustainable Housing in a Mixed Market

The global financial crisis has put increasing pressure on the European housing market. Not only are investors finding it increasingly hard to access the requisite capital to help solve the problem of a lack of housing delivery in a fragile market, but consumer trends have also fundamentally changed. More consumers are now choosing to rent property for longer periods because of the flexibility that such an arrangement offers. The shift toward relatively unstable employment patterns in the postcrisis economy means that consumers have more desire for higher-quality and flexible rented accommodations.

Given the shift in consumer behavior and real estate investors' difficulty in accessing cheap credit, there needs to be more focus on encouraging institutional investment in the European residential real estate market. The investment opportunity available to institutions needs to be clarified and the investment climate made more welcoming. Residential real estate investment trusts (REITs), the relaxation of discouraging tax legislation (such as Stamp Duty Land Tax in the United Kingdom), and the simplification of planning laws would all help to encourage greater institutional investment.

In terms of improving the sustainability of housing throughout Europe, there is a necessity to substantially increase investment both in retrofitting of existing housing stock and in new building. Pilot projects for energy-efficient affordable and social housing have been successfully driven by standards such as PassivHaus in Germany, MINERGIE-P in Switzerland, and Zero Carbon Homes in the United Kingdom but are not yet mainstream. European targets for carbon and greenhouse gas emissions reduction already go some way to encourage this investment, but confusion around multiple standards, energy efficiency certification, and complex legislation is hampering large-scale change. The European Commission is investing heavily in further research into "Near or Net Zero Energy" (NZE) buildings and exploring the findings of such initiatives as the Sustainable Urban Metabolism for Europe project.

2. Work in Growing New Industries, as well as Traditional Strengths

While abandoning traditional economic strengths is not a development strategy on any community's agenda, the leaders of Europe's cities must reassess how their existing composition of employment must evolve in the new economic milieu of rapid globalization. Trends in technology, as well as the need to move toward more low-carbon business activities, provide Europe's highly skilled workforce with an opportunity. Europe is well placed to exploit burgeoning strengths in sectors such as low-carbon and environmental goods and services, commercial services, information technologies, advanced manufacturing, and the life sciences. These growing new industries are based on innovation and knowledge. Accordingly, Europe's cities must place greater emphasis on attracting and retaining talent, because a highly skilled workforce will undoubtedly be one of

Similar to the German PassivHaus standard, MINERGIE-P is a Swiss standard for low energy consumption in new and refurbished homes. This single-family home in Vordemwald, Switzerland, earned the label by drawing its heat and hot water from heat pumps, geothermal probes, and photovoltaic systems.

MINERGIE BUILDING AGENCY

the most important factors contributing to city success over the next decade.

Competition for talented individuals is fierce, and payment is far from the only concern for knowledge workers. There is a developing trend toward overall quality of life being the primary consideration for potential employees of companies. Firms are aware of this trend, and it is up to cities to create the right environment, where companies will happily invest in the city, knowing that they will be able to attract the best talent. More companies are also becoming aware that their brand image and approach to issues such as carbon emissions are increasingly being considered by prospective employees.

3. Invest in New Assets that Are Globally Competitive

One of the first cuts that Europe's manufacturing companies made as a result of the global financial crisis was in the area of research and development. Moving forward, however, Europe needs to focus on developing its strengths, and in a knowledge worker age, these strengths lie in human resources and innovation. Although competition with the world's emerging economies will be fierce, early and substantial investment in education, research and development, and innovative business practices will put Europe in a strong position to overcome its global competitors.

The European Commission's Europe 2020 strategy both acknowledges these trends and sets appropriate targets to take advantage of these identified opportunities. Indeed, the strategy targets 3 percent of the EU's GDP (public and private) to be invested in research and development, and innovation by 2020. The strategy also recognizes that continued investment in skills will be critical to Europe maintaining its competitive edge. Two targets are to reduce school dropout rates below 10 percent and to have at least 40 percent of 30 to 34 year olds completing third-level education by 2020.

The new economic norm in Europe is one of constrained credit and low demand, with concentrated investment in skills and innovative industries, Europe's businesses must strive to enhance their reputation as a preferred supplier to emerging economies. Both the public and private sectors must work in synergy to ensure that growing firms have access to finance, world class innovation, science and research, and the material and digital infrastructures that they require.

4. Connect with Growth Opportunity

If Europe's cities wish to be internationally competitive, they must find new ways to invest in infrastructure development. In the new economic climate, Europe's cities cannot be as reliant as they once were on government finance to improve their own infrastructure. Mixed-finance infrastructure development projects need to become increasingly common. In Paris, for example, the Grand Paris Plan is concerned with ensuring that the economic centers that make up the eight counties in the Paris region are connected. Connectivity will be facilitated through the region's 15-year transport strategy with a budget of €32.4 billion. The improvement of the public transport network, the Greater Paris Express, will be financed through a mixture of state, local government, and public/private partnership funding. The network will also ensure that the region's urban centers, suburbs, and airports are all within easy reach.

Transport infrastructure between European cities is also increasingly important to the successful operation of the European single market and has been recognized in the Lisbon Competitiveness Strategy as well as the Europe 2020 Strategy. Traffic between EU member states is expected to double by 2020, with over €1.5 trillion of investment required between 2010 and 2030 to meet these needs. The European Union is supporting the TEN-T implementation through several financial instruments: the TEN-T program, the Cohesion Fund, the European Regional Development Fund, and European Investment Bank's loans and credit guarantees.

5. Engage with Europe's Neighbors to Increase Scale and Opportunity

While Europe's cities should be orienting themselves globally to take advantage of the opportunities offered by emerging markets, they must also engage more with Europe's immediate neighbors, to increase the scale and opportunity of economic activity. Economic trading relationships with Russia and Turkey especially could provide some of the biggest growth markets for European businesses over the next decade. An improvement in the relationship between Russia, Turkey, and the European Commission may be fraught with economic and political challenges, but the successful negotiation of these challenges could be the key to improving the future of Europe's overall economic outlook. While the EU's relationship with Russia is largely based on energy, the large and growing Russian market is already attracting substantial European investment in consumer industries, while Turkey's relative economic vitality and its political segue into the Islamic world should be further explored by Europe's cities and businesses over the next decade.

6. Lead the World in Energy Efficiency and Sustainable Development

For Europe to maintain its global lead in energy efficiency and sustainable development over the next decade requires significant investment, but the potential rewards could be substantial. The European Commission's Europe 2020 Strategy targets reducing greenhouse gas emissions by 20 percent over those of 1990; increasing the share of renewables in final energy consumption to 20 percent; and moving toward a 20 percent increase in energy efficiency by 2020. If Europe works toward achieving these targets, it is estimated that it could reduce the cost of Europe's oil and gas imports by €60 billion by 2020. Further integration of the European energy market could boost GDP by 0.6 percent to 0.8 percent. The consequence of this investment could be transformational to the success of Europe's economy, while giving Europe's green companies the competitive edge that they require to stave off competition from the United States and China in these sectors.

The global financial crisis and ensuing Great Recession in the United States places urban economics on a new course. In the United States, homeownership will adjust downward to the low 60 percent range, as it ramps up significantly in Asia. Credit and lending will return to recognizable standards, neither ridiculously loose nor so tight. The large demographic groups, Gen Y and Boomers, will drive changes in consumer preferences and dominate market activity. A rising middle class in Asia will both create new markets and bring in new market participants. Europe will struggle, as some lagging cities experience shrinking and stronger cities try to accommodate new immigrants with reasonable jobs and affordable housing.

And yet, it will be different.

The complexity of the global capital markets and the sheer pace of change across communities will be a compelling test of leadership. Public and private, corporate and personal, how we meet the future will demand new ideas and new skills. Flexibility, agility, creative analytics, and problem solving are mandatory. Within real estate, a greater emphasis will be placed on assessing broader market characteristics, not just the spreadsheet for the proposed project. While the action will be urban and metropolitan, the appeal of closer-in properties will outweigh the increasingly faint memory of the ease associated with past greenfield growth at the metropolitan perimeter.

In hindsight, the recent global recession and the U.S. housing bust mark an inflection point for adjusting attitudes and behaviors, just as separate demographic, technological, and global economic forces gain a cumulative transformational momentum. **The real estate world is hurtling into a different place and time. Change is coming at a faster pace with more uncertain consequences. Success will take on different forms and risks will increase. Standing pat or ignoring new realities is not possible. Notably, investment will gravitate to places that welcome business and view public investments—in education, infrastructure, and innovation—as prerequisites for progress and economic sustainability.**

The complexity of the global capital markets and the sheer pace of change across communities will be a **compelling test of leadership.**

What's Next?

Looking ahead, new riptides crisscross real estate markets:

1. **Less is Better.** Tenants and owners across all property sectors squeeze more out of every square foot. But efficiency means more than shrinking space per capita to save costs and lowering utility bills. It's about creating environments that feed productive interaction in the workplace and satisfy social connections at home. Space adds value if it's multidimensional and adaptable, and can sustain greater intensity of use.

2. **Discovering New Market Segments.** Markets become ever more segmented and specialized—one size certainly no longer fits all. Investors and developers become more sophisticated in "getting closer to the market" and meeting fragmenting demand, which varies within neighborhoods, from city to suburb, and from region to region. Shopping centers target different immigrant communities and age groups. Companies refine location strategies to attract younger talent and move closer to global pathways. Housing demands diverge among splintering household types. Expanding cohorts like intergenerational families, single women living alone, Gen Y couples, and Boomer empty nesters all pursue different lifestyles, while traditional nuclear families seem ever less dominant.

3. **Some Sip Champagne While Others Drink Beer.** Wealth and purchasing power concentrate in a smaller sliver of society and these affluents cluster on wealth islands—typically familiar prime districts and neighborhoods in gateway markets or resort communities. Meeting this profitable upper-crust market requires creative projects that redefine the "flight to quality" mindset—in comfort, safety, and luxury. Not surprisingly, more space is no object for these buyers. By contrast, the need for workforce housing grows due to underlying demographics. The development margins in these projects could decrease, since average worker incomes remain under stress from global competition and automation. Public sector cuts leave communities and regions scrambling to finance low-income rental development as the churn of foreclosures diminishes upward mobility.

4. **Creating Jobs or High-Quality Employment?** Ongoing globalization, the evolving information economy, and advanced manufacturing create new jobs in different places, pressure down wages or eliminate work in old-line industries, and require advanced skills as well as enhanced education backgrounds. The graying population, meanwhile, needs more highly paid doctors and even more low-wage caregivers. Real estate players must keep up with topsy-turvy change, favoring urban areas anchored with concentrations of brainpower jobs and nurtured by major academic institutions. As the public sector grapples to find solutions for the long-term unemployed, Internet commerce companies may suddenly seek space for thousands of new employees, Chinese construction conglomerates may enter the U.S. infrastructure market, and German cars manufactured in South Carolina may get exported back to Europe. U.S. and European property developers and urban planners could find their best opportunities outside the country.

5. **C2C (City to City).** Global rates of urbanization reach their steepest growth curves in history: nearly 500 million more people will live in cities over the next decade, and 60 percent of the world population will settle in urban areas. Here is where business, commerce, and wealth creation happen. In the United States alone, metropolitan areas generate 80 percent of the nation's jobs and GDP. Expect international C2C networks to form, creating new economies and conceivably a new geopolitical power structure, serviced along increasingly well-traveled global pathways. The economic significance of C2C makes "sister city" initiatives look like Girl Scouts.

6. **The City Mouse and the Country Mouse.** Cities and surrounding rural areas grow farther apart in the nightly televised fight over public resources. Political rancor intensifies in states where city mice demand more of the cheese (to invest in infrastructure) which sustains the regional economy, while entrenched country mice battle to keep their historic share of the benefits. Jurisdictions—and their communities—do better by eliminating the regional competition over attracting new business and tax base and instead pool resources to integrate land use planning with regional transport networks that improve

mobility and create dynamic 24-hour commercial centers. This approach positions each local government to attract more private partners to help finance and build new projects with enduring community value. Slow-moving democracies come head to head with more fast-moving albeit less participatory international governments.

7. **Real Estate Remains a Tradable Asset Class.** Large institutional investors and pension funds continue to seek high-quality real estate product. With less being built, the opportunity to reposition, retenant, and upgrade existing assets finds broad receptivity. The Class A assets in prime gateway markets and those assets directly related to educational, medical, or federal anchors gain favor. Equity investors become even more attuned to global markets and more sophisticated at conducting structured finance transactions.

8. **Capturing Value in Waste.** Buildings represent a goldmine of waste—solids, fluids, heat—that steadily adds up on tenant and owner balance sheets in higher utility bills and carting charges. The real estate industry finds the tools to capture value in simply reducing waste—not only by employing more efficient building systems, but also by changing lease terms and financial instruments to discourage profligate behaviors. In a lackluster economy, eliminating waste represents one of the lowest-risk investment strategies to create positive returns.

9. **Information Is Capital.** All elements of the built environment connect to a series of digital networks, enabling more precise management of buildings, equipment, and program uses. Look for a firehose of data that enables a new generation of real estate services to crop up, brokering virtually anything across

the built environment in close to real time. Want to drill deeper into the neighborhood market data? Need to negotiate your way through the next brownout? Want to rent out a spare bedroom for one night? How about an initial public offering for that idea? You can now do it—all on a smart phone or with a new app.

10. **Beware of the Black Swans.** We cannot predict them because we do not know what they are. But they are there, lurking, ready to upset the markets. It could be a quick flash or a slow, unrecognizable trend, but whatever they are, we know they are coming. Maybe.

Acknowledgments

Contributing Authors

Jonathan D. Miller, Primary Author

Maureen L. McAvey,
Executive Vice President,
ULI Initiatives Group

Uwe Brandes, Senior Vice President,
ULI Initiatives Group

C.Y. Leung, Chairman, ULI Asia
(Asia Outlook)

Gareth Evans, Inside Cities
(Europe Outlook)

Greg Clark, Senior Fellow,
ULI EMEA/India

We deeply appreciate the input, insight, and participation of ULI trustees, members, and staff who participated in the dialogues and meetings used to create this publication.

ULI Senior Executives

Patrick Phillips
Chief Executive Officer

Cheryl Cummins
Executive Officer

Michael Terseck
Chief Financial Officer/Chief
Administrative Officer

Richard M. Rosan
President, ULI Foundation

Joe Montgomery
Chief Executive, Europe

David Howard
Executive Vice President,
Development and ULI Foundation

Maureen McAvey
Executive Vice President, Initiatives

Lela Agnew
Executive Vice President,
Communications

ULI Project Staff

Maureen McAvey
Executive Vice President, Initiatives

Uwe S. Brandes
Senior Vice President, Initiatives

Matthew F. Johnston
Research Manager

Sarah Nemecek
Research Associate

Stephanie Ball
Research Assistant

Darby Parker
Research Assistant

Alexandra Notay
Vice President, Strategic Programmes,
ULI Europe

John Fitzgerald
Vice President, Director, ULI Asia

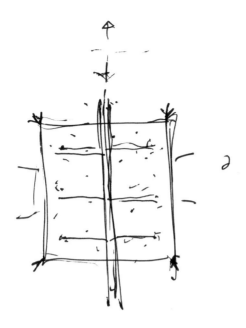

ULI Senior Resident Fellows

Stephen R. Blank
Senior Resident Fellow
Finance and Capital Markets

Michael Horst
Senior Resident Fellow
Leadership

John K. McIlwain
Senior Resident Fellow
J. Ronald Terwilliger Chair for
Housing

Edward T. McMahon
Senior Resident Fellow
ULI/Charles Fraser Chair for
Sustainable Development

Tom Murphy
Senior Resident Fellow
Joseph C. Canizaro/Klingbeil Family
Chair for Urban Development

Greg Clark
Senior Fellow
ULI EMEA/India

ULI Production Staff

James Mulligan
Managing Editor

Lise Lingo
Publications Professionals LLC
Manuscript Editor

Betsy VanBuskirk
Creative Director

Anne Morgan
Graphic Designer

Craig Chapman
Senior Director, Publishing Operations

TRF 1998 Bond 246 millic
WADA - 305 -
0.5 million - bureau of Reclamation for waste water reuse
MTA - 30 million.
2.7 million ACF

Suburban
timeline

Town
county

750   1995   2000

EFFICIENCY PRODUCES VALUE:

EFFICIENT L.V. releases disposable
and municipal income.

Bellfine   2.8 million total
$140 million in Park Imp. Bonds, Cap. improvements
                        program fund
            Dept of Watershed Management
TAD - 1.7 billion.
143 million state/local grants.
(37 million for private sorns